Marketing
UNCOVERED

Careers Uncovered guides aim to expose the truth about what it's really like to work in a particular field, containing unusual and thought-provoking facts about the profession you are interested in. Written in a lively and accessible style, *Careers Uncovered* guides explore the highs and lows of the career, along with the job opportunities and skills and qualities you will need to help you make your way forward.

Titles in this series include:

Accountancy Uncovered
Charity and Voluntary Work Uncovered
Design Uncovered
E-Commerce Uncovered
The Internet Uncovered
Journalism Uncovered, 2nd edition
Law Uncovered, 2nd edition
Media Uncovered
Medicine Uncovered, 2nd edition
Music Industry Uncovered, 2nd edition
Nursing and Midwifery Uncovered
Performing Arts Uncovered
Psychology Uncovered
Sport and Fitness Uncovered, 2nd edition
Teaching Uncovered
The Travel Industry Uncovered
Working for Yourself Uncovered

trotman

Marketing UNCOVERED

2nd edition

Amy Robertson

Marketing Uncovered

This 2nd edition published in 2009 by Trotman Publishing, an imprint of Crimson Publishing, Westminster House, Kew Road, Richmond, Surrey TW9 2ND.

© Trotman Publishing 2009

Author: Andi Robertson

First edition published as *Marketing and PR Uncovered* by Catherine Harris in 2003 by Trotman & Company Ltd.

British Library Cataloguing Publication Data
A catalogue record for this book is available from the British Library

ISBN: 978-1-84455-200-9

Typeset by RefineCatch Limited, Bungay, Suffolk

Printed and bound in Italy by LEGO SpA

Contents

About the author

Andi Robertson was born in South Devon in 1959 and educated at Kingsbridge School. He set up his own marketing and sales consultancy business in 1982. After 22 years of sales and management experience in London and then back home in Devon, he opted for a change of career and became a mature student. Getting a BA and the Certificate of Education enabled him to become a business advisor and lecturer.

In 2001 Andi was diagnosed with Parkinson's disease, and a combination of personal and professional interest fuelled subsequent research and the establishment of the Disabled Entrepreneurs Project which helps disabled people start up their own business.

He has also written articles on marketing, disability and small business issues for regional newspapers and national magazines and has won two small prizes for his short stories. In October 2006 his first book, *Working for Yourself Uncovered*, was published by Trotman.

Travelling has always featured in Andi's life but he was always delighted to come home to the South Hams (Devon) where he was born, grew up and lives with his wife, Jane. They have four children: Laura, Rosie, Charli and Alex.

To see more of Andi's writing visit www.holmeconsultants.co.uk.

Acknowledgements

Thanks to my wife Jane for all her love and support and to Maggie Lewis, without her hard work and support this book may never have been written.

Preface

My mum didn't like marketing. She was a traditionalist and would probably have preferred her son to be a doctor. This wasn't a problem; in fact we teased each other about it. We didn't really mention my job much. I didn't mind; we had plenty of other things to talk about.

In the 1980s mum became seriously ill, so I drove down to Devon from London to see her as much as I could. On one occasion on a sunny summer's day I found her in bed, very poorly. We talked. It was great to see her. I mentioned the fact that I had been offered a new marketing job. I kept it brief because she was clearly getting tired and needed to take a nap.

'I know you're not crazy about marketing,' I said, standing up and smiling. Mum smiled back at me and, as her eyes closed, she opened her mouth to say something. I leaned forward to hear what she had to say. 'Froth!' she breathed, winked at me and fell asleep in an instant. She'd had the last word.

I poured myself a cold Guinness, grabbed a book and went to the veranda to sit in the sun and read. An hour passed, eventually Mum woke up and I wandered into her room, glass in hand, to find out if she'd like a cup of tea. By way of a joke she answered this question by somehow snatching the glass out of my hand and taking a great swig of Guinness. This was something of a surprise because my mother was not one to swig anything, and she certainly didn't drink Guinness.

Unfortunately for her the Guinness had been sitting in the sun and was quite flat and warm, indeed it must have tasted really bad if the expression on her face was anything to go by. We were both seized by a laughing fit that went on for some minutes. When we thought it was over one of us would start the other off again. I remember that moment well.

'That Guinness has been in the sun for hours, its flat!' I gasped.

'It's disgusting,' mum said between bursts of laughter.

'Know why?' I spluttered, drying my eyes and hers.

'No, why?'

'No froth!' I said.

We both were overwhelmed with laughter. It took some time to recover.

When I got back to London I was soon in the thick of it at work. A couple of days later a letter arrived and when I opened it I found a small card with my Mum's spidery hand writing on it. It said, 'Good luck with the froth'.

Andi Robertson

Introduction

This is a personal interpretation of the business of marketing that draws upon the experiences of myself and others over the last 30 years. I'm not an academic and this is not a text book, there are plenty of those around already, I am trying to help the budding marketer make an informed career decision.

Let's look briefly at what *Marketing Uncovered* is all about.

Chapter One provides us with an overview of the industry, with definitions and comments on some fundamental misconceptions. I also offer an explanation as to how marketing fits into the business life cycle with an outline of marketing tools and external market forces.

Chapter Two explains how different marketing activities translate into jobs and how these jobs fit in to different disciplines of marketing such as advertising, direct sales, research and so on. The narrative provides the reader with statistics and figures on how many people are employed, what income they are likely to receive, and how the business is changing with the ever widening possibilities that technology and IT bring to the role of marketing.

Chapter Three introduces us to Ben and his marketing campaign for the Widget. Here we study the tools of the marketer's trade.

Chapter Four looks at what skills and attributes might be needed for different types of marketing jobs that you will be faced with at all levels of the career ladder. I raise questions to help the reader assess what particular talents they possess, and have tried to help readers consider where they might fit in. I have also included diary entries drawn from the experience of real marketers to illustrate the sort of thing you might be faced with in the very near future.

Chapter Five provides information about training and qualifications, from leaving school to membership of the professional bodies.

Chapter Six is about real marketers. This chapter contains transcripts of interviews with experienced people from research, advertising, IT, direct sales, the small business sector and event management. These people have all spoken frankly about their past, how they got into the business, what they enjoyed, what they didn't enjoy, and they have kindly provided advice for any readers who are thinking of becoming marketers. I hope the immediacy and the frankness of what has been said in these interviews communicates itself effectively to you all. I've tried not to interfere. I think the words of successful marketers speak for themselves.

Useful resources, references and contact details are listed at the end of the book.

Chapter One

WHAT IS MARKETING AND WHAT IS THE STATE OF THE SECTOR?

The first thing we need to do is nail the 'what is marketing?' question. Because once you are clear about what marketers do, you can decide which part of the marketing process interests you most and push on with your marketing career.

Essentially, marketing is a communication process which enables people and communities of all descriptions to discover, and buy, both current and new products and services that will satisfy their needs and desires.

One of the best definitions comes from Adcock et al. (2001), lecturers at Coventry and Warwick universities, who said, 'Marketing is about getting the right goods (or services) in the right quantity, to the right place, at the right time and making a profit out of the operation.'

Marketing has many different functions that vary at different stages of the business life cycle. For instance, research will be carried out by marketers at the early stages of a product or service's life. Marketers will be responsible for the efficient distribution of what is being sold and this in my view includes the promotional activity (namely sales) that the majority of companies will use to achieve their objectives. Not everybody agrees with me, but I take the view in these pages that the sales department is an integral part of the marketing process.

GOOD MARKETING

You don't have to just take my word for it. There is plenty of evidence that many of the movers and shakers in the world of business appreciate what good marketing will do for their company. Lee Iacocca, an American businessman most commonly known for his revival of the Chrysler Corporation in the 1980s, took the view that having good ideas is one thing 'but if you cannot get them across, your ideas will not get you anywhere'.

The search for a satisfactory answer to the 'what is marketing?' question is hampered by the fact that the word marketing, like the word strategy, is regularly shoehorned into sentences by anyone who wishes to appear businesslike.

This means that you can now see the word marketing being used over and over again when a more specific term would have added clarity to what was being said.

In the words of Joe Saxton, chair of Charity Communications, 'Marketing is probably the single most abused and misused word.' He continued,

Figure 1 Good marketing outcomes

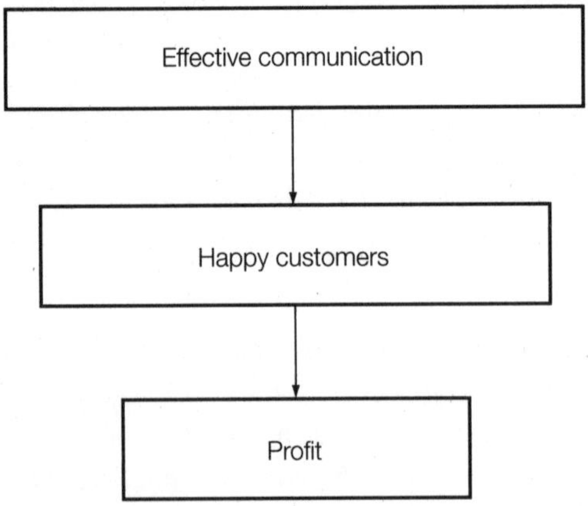

Effective communication

↓

Happy customers

↓

Profit

'We have a Head of Marketing – this particular title could be a fundraising role, a branding role, a communications role or a services role.'

This misuse of the word marketing has clouded not just the understanding of its meaning but also its importance to UK commerce. However, this misuse hasn't put off the many influential fans of marketing, as you can see from the quotes below.

'Half the money I spend on advertising is wasted, and the problem is I do not know which half.'
Lord Leverhulme 1851–1925, British philanthropist and founder of Unilever (in Ogilvy (1980))

'For a business not to advertise is like winking at a girl in the dark. You know what you are doing but no one else does.'
Attributed to Steuart H. Britt, US advertising consultant

'Unless your campaign has a big idea, it will pass like a ship in the night.'
David Ogilvy, (Ogilvy (1980)). See Chapter Six for more about David Ogilvy

'Marketing takes a lifetime to master.'
Philip Kotler, US marketing guru (Kotler (2003))

Finding a fan of marketing is one thing, finding a satisfactory definition of marketing is another. Some of the better ones concentrate on the process of satisfying customer needs. Philip Kotler, an American professor once described as 'the world's foremost expert on the strategic practice of marketing', described marketing as 'the social and managerial process by which individuals and groups obtain what they want and need through creating, offering and exchanging products of value with others'; and the Chartered Institute of Marketing (CIM) rather neatly explains marketing as the 'management process to identify this anticipates and satisfies customer requirements profitably'.

Trying to pin down the state of the marketing sector is not easy because of the pace of change; and yes you've guessed it, if marketing itself is always changing then so are the definitions. So let's check out some of the new ones.

The American Marketing Association (AMA) states

> *'Marketing is an organizational function and a set of processes for creating, communicating and delivering value to customers and for managing customer relationships in ways that benefit the organization and its stakeholders'*

The Chartered Institute of Marketing (CIM) has acknowledged the changing times and has revised its 30 year old definition, proposing to define marketing as

> *'a business function that creates value by stimulating, facilitating and fulfilling customer demand. It does this by building brands, nurturing innovation, developing relationships, creating good customer service and communicating benefits. With a customer-centric view, marketing brings positive return on investment, satisfies shareholders and stakeholders from business and the community, and contributes to positive behavioural change and a sustainable business future.'*

> *(CIM 2006)*

This definition still describes the same aims, but reflects the different ways in which they might be accomplished given these new economic and technological times.

So we know that marketing is essentially a term used broadly to cover many aspects of a company's brand, advertising and promotional strategies and the process of identifying customer needs, looking at how to meet them and the best way to generate profit. So much for definitions, let's look at the functions of marketing. Let's see what marketing people do.

If you are an accountant, some might say it's easy to describe what you do. For instance, the financial year is over, and the books are passed to the accountant who prepares a set of accounts for the taxman. Nice and simple. (OK simplistic!) You won't be surprised to hear that describing what the marketer does is more difficult.

Take a look at Figure 2. This illustrates the development of many businesses as they mature through the four stages. You will see that marketing has a number of quite different roles.

When a product or service is at the design stage marketing researchers might target some focus groups to pinpoint what this kind of market segment will be receptive to.

When the product or service is launched the advertising department will swing into action, and when it needs to be sold, sales teams will hit the streets and the telephones and internet, while customer service teams deal with problems and complaints.

The functions of marketing weave their way through the life of the business or product and the marketing department deals with these tasks as and when they occur, and a marketing specialist deals with a particular function like advertising or PR on a permanent basis.

The diagram illustrates key indicators of success or failure (ie turnover, profit) and activity (in this case marketing activity such as research, distribution, sales) during the life of a particular product or service. What follows is an attempt to illustrate how the role of the marketer will vary during this period of time.

Figure 2 Marketing activity

Early years Start up High investment Low profits	Consolidation Rapid growth Greatest profits	Maturity Period of maturity Sales maximised Profit weakens	Decline Market saturation Decline commences

Research
Design

Advertising

Customer service

Cyber marketing

PR

Direct sales/mail

Distribution

Other marketing functions
(eg pricing merchandising)

Enough of marketing activity, lets talk about parties. Can you explain what different marketers do in the context of being at a party? Yes you can!

You see the boss of a big marketing agency at a party.
You go up to her and say, 'I'm a fantastic Marketer.'
That's Direct Marketing

You're at a party with a bunch of friends and see the boss of a big marketing agency. One of your friends goes up to her and pointing at you says, 'He's a fantastic marketer.'
That's Advertising

You're at a party and you see the boss of a big marketing agency. You go up to her and get her telephone number. The next day you call and say, 'Hi, I'm a fantastic marketer.'
That's Telemarketing

You're at a party and you see the boss of a big marketing agency. You get up and straighten your tie; you walk up to her and pour her a drink. You open the door for her, pick up her bag after she drops it, offer her a ride, and then say, 'By the way, I'm a fantastic marketer.'
That's Public Relations

You're at a party and you see the boss of a big marketing agency. She walks up to you and says, 'I hear you're a fantastic marketer.'
That's Brand Recognition

Marketers have a broad range of promotional activities to choose from, in fact the sky is quite literally the limit: I know of a night club owner who spent a fortune having an aeroplane banner flown up and down the coast over the crowded Spanish beaches one summer, while another client of mine hired someone to stand in the rain outside a tube station with a sandwich board around his neck.

Either of these activities may benefit your company and may even meet with some success. The checklist below is not exhaustive but it illustrates just some of the many different promotional activities that the marketer has at his or her disposal. Having done the preparation, such as market and product research, the task of the marketer is to cherry pick the marketing methods that would fit best into their strategy and to build these activities into a campaign which is both practical and imaginative enough to achieve their goals.

WHAT ARE THE OPTIONS?

- Advertise in catalogues and business directories, newspapers (national or local, including free press), on radio and TV, brochures, magazines, and trade journals.

- Get editorial coverage in any of the above by distributing press releases.

- Advertise in the shop windows, on posters, billboards, sandwich boards and your own vans or aeroplane banners.

- Use e-marketing – via your own website or advertising on other people's websites.

- Distribute leaflets through doors in areas where you think there may be potential customers (known as a 'leaflet drop').

- Send out direct mail marketing– either by post or via the internet.

- Organise a direct sales campaign (cold calling).

- Attend/exhibit at trade fairs.

- Organise your own promotional event.

- Give promotional talks.

- Sponsor an event or product.

- Organise a competition.

- Offer promotional gifts (known as merchandising).

- Offer discounts, special offers and bargains – eg 'buy one get one free' offers (known in the trade as 'BOGOFs') and loss leaders (which draw the customers in to buy, although they are priced to make a loss).

■ Work with other businesses to help each other – known as 'partnership marketing'.

■ Create referrers ('centres of influence') by building good relationships with customers and supply/distribution chains.

■ Network and gain contacts and recommendations by word of mouth.

■ Cross selling – using one product to help promote another.

And many more!

Outside influences – market forces

There is a bigger picture to consider, one that contains what we shall refer to as market forces such as:

■ the economy (eg new budget initiatives)

■ social circumstances (eg environmental issues like global warming)

■ political decisions (eg policy decisions such as election pledges).

They can change everything and often do.

Many a marketing professional has come to grief because they did not consider the bigger picture or the marketing environment. This bigger picture is home to market forces which can stop your campaign for the product in its tracks and seriously dent your career.

I remember hearing a story about a marketer who meticulously planned the launch of a brand-new alcopop just before a barrage of adverse publicity hit the airwaves following stories of binge drinking among underage drinkers in our high streets and market towns. The market force in this case was the growing public belief that companies apparently target young drinkers.

'Authentic marketing is not the art of selling what you make but knowing what to make. It is the art of identifying and understanding customer needs and creating solutions that deliver satisfaction to the customers, profits to the producers and benefits for the stakeholders.'

Philip Kotler (Kotler (1988))

The marketing environment contains many factors that could, if you don't pay proper attention to them, spell the ruin of a carefully planned campaign. These factors could be environmental, legal, social, economic, technological or political. The pneumonic PESTLE is a way of remembering what the market forces are.

Market forces

These should be considered as part of any marketer's research when, for instance planning a product launch.

Political	Change in Government
	Policy changes eg health
	Interest rates
Economic	Minimum wage
	Redundancies
	Workforce movement eg forces
Social	Leisure time
	Sport
	Fashion
	Double glazing
Techno	Communications
	IT
	Equipment/machinery
Legal	Changes in legislation
	Currency changes
	Insurance increases
Environmental	Waste management
	Save trees
	Green issues

Even Henry Ford fell foul of market forces when he tried to launch his pride and joy, the new Edsel car, on 4 September 1957. Amid much fanfare and hype the launch campaign failed to inspire his sceptical customers and it ground to a halt. This failure is still discussed, but the general consensus is that Ford didn't have its finger on the pulse of what Americans wanted. Ford thought that technology would carry the day but social forces dictated otherwise; $400,000,000 and two years later the Edsel was discontinued.

Coca-Cola, like Henry Ford, failed to spot a social trend in the form of the public's changing taste buds. Their new flat-tasting and overly sugary Coke's advertising campaign lost its fizz, forcing Coca-Cola to switch back to their original formula.

A classical technological market force brought the house down at a Microsoft press event when audience members were treated to the sight of Windows 98 crashing before their very eyes as Bill Gates laughingly said, 'That must be why were not shipping Windows 98 yet.'

Numerous other examples exist of wars and recessions – for instance killing off new product launches, and campaigns being stopped in their tracks by legal and environmental pressures. You may forget PESTLE but it won't forget you.

I have tried in the pages of this first chapter to give you a flavour of marketing theory and its relevance in today's workplace. If you want to learn more about theory, there are other books to read – see the resource section for details.

This book is now going in a different direction because we're going to talk about the marketing industry today and what roles exist for those who choose marketing as a career.

Chapter Two

HOW DOES MARKETING WORK? WHAT ARE THE ROLES WITHIN THE INDUSTRY?

Chapter One outlined the kind of activities that marketers do but, you may ask, who does them? Where? And for what reward?

Because the definition of marketing is so broad, there are a wide variety of roles in this field of work. It has been estimated that between 550,000 and 600,000 people in the UK work directly in marketing, while some 750,000 are full-time sales people who will undertake some marketing related activities. And I know that many other people often do some marketing work for their employer without even realising it!

To complicate things further, marketing may be done in-house or out-sourced to a specialist agency. Any organisation, private sector, public sector or not-for-profit, must market its products or services. Only larger companies will be able to support their own marketing department, but the reality is that many people in an organisation will have some marketing responsibility, especially those in customer contact positions.

The most obvious place to identify marketing is by someone with 'sales' or 'marketing' in their job title, but many other senior and junior positions will find themselves promoting the company in different ways. Imagine you work for a small company. Inevitably your job description will be fairly loose and flexible: 'any other duties that may be required' is often included in a formal description, but actually applies to most jobs. You may be called on to phone a potential customer to set up an appointment, you could be asked to send emails to customers about changes to the company's services, you may have to organise a company event (see the PA's story in Chapter Five). All of these are marketing. On the other hand, if you are asked to organise an advert for a new product, you may call on the services of a graphic designer or an advertising agency. You may have to do it yourself. Marketing is everywhere!

WHO DOES WHAT?

While the principles of marketing remain the same over time, the job of the marketer will inevitably change with technological advances. However, I have gathered together some figures to give an indication of what an entrant to the marketing world may expect. These figures are a guide based on a moment in time, and will obviously change as economic conditions and technology impact on how the sector works.

Figures produced by the Marketing and Sales Standards Setting Body (MSSSB) suggest that marketing strategy and planning (eg mapping out in a marketing plan what the various departments of a particular company will be expected to contribute during the promotion of a product or service) are the most important activities, and these are usually carried out in-house. This represents the top level, company specific decision making that directors and managers do.

They are closely followed in order of importance by customer relationship management (CRM) (the interface between customers and the business, and ensuring relationship is maintained well), and product or brand management (ie control of all aspects of a product such as Virgin Cola, or a brand such as all Virgin products and services). CRM is also usually done in-house, because it is so integrated in the day to day running of the business. However, while the decisions about product and brand management may be taken by company directors, they may well be advised by specialist consultants.

Only around 50% of organisations undertake direct sales in-house, while others use an agency for it. The activities most likely to be undertaken with help from an agency are advertising, communications and market research.

Figure 3 Interaction between in-house and external marketers

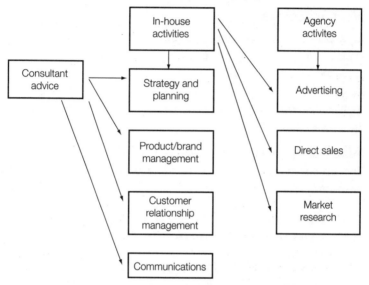

The following statistics give a good impression of the current state of the marketing industry.

■ Age – Marketing is a relatively youthful occupation: around 75% of those working in marketing are aged between 25 and 45 years, and if you are aiming for the higher rungs of the marketing career ladder, such as marketing director or senior marketing manager, you are likely to reach them by age 40.

■ Sex – The Marketing Rewards survey 2008 found that 63% of those working in the marketing sector are men and only 20% of marketing directors are women. Their pay is 18% lower than their male counterparts. The MSSSB figures suggest that women are slightly more likely to become managers in an agency.

■ Sector – Nearly 30% of marketers are employed in the public sector, 38% in manufacturing, 20% in the private sector, 5% in the voluntary sector, and 7% as consultants.

WHO EMPLOYS MARKETERS?

Marketing can be done by in-house teams, or by a consultant or agency. An organisation may even use both. So, let's take a look at where you might find different activities.

Market sectors

In the private, commercial sector, the use of marketing is the most obvious. Whether retail or wholesale, organisations are primarily trying to persuade customers to buy their products or services. On the smallest scale, we all market ourselves when we set about getting a job, right up to the multi-national company selling computers, soft drinks or financial services across the globe.

Public sector organisations use marketing to promote their services to us. They inform, educate and encourage us to adopt certain behaviours, use a service or take up a particular benefit.

A political party markets itself to the electorate, and then the Government tries to influence our behaviour to achieve the aims of its manifesto.

Charities have a two pronged marketing purpose: to raise awareness of their cause, make us care about it, and donate to it; and then, having used the money, to tell us about their achievements and encourage us to continue supporting them.

Any organisation, private sector, public sector or not-for-profit, is likely to perform the following activities, either by designated marketing professionals or by other members of staff.

In-house marketing activities

■ Strategic marketing – someone determines how marketing can contribute to achieving the organisation's objectives so an individual responsible for marketing strategy will put together the overall marketing plan and then oversee its implementation. This may be the marketing director.

■ Coordinating day-to-day activities within a company.

Individual management of a particular product or brand

■ Market analysis – undertaking market research, analysing the results and using them. For example, to forecast demand, or to assess the effectiveness of marketing activity and brand awareness.

■ Marketing communications – co-ordinating communications with potential and current customers/users. This role is of particular significance in the public sector and not-for-profit organisations, where information is effectively the 'product'. Communication may be across many media: print, TV, radio, internet/email, direct mail.

■ Customer relationship management – a specialism that has expanded with the development of software that spans organisations to capture information and present it in a form that makes proactive contact more targeted and easier to achieve.

You could work for a specialist agency, which may concentrate on one area: advertising, market research, direct sales, or provide all these services. They may offer advice on a consultancy basis, or carry out the activities themselves.

Marketing agency activities

Advertising

■ Account management – acting as the interface between the client and the agency, and leading the agency team in their activities.

■ Account planning – using market research and analysis, and the client's brief to work out a marketing strategy.

■ Media planning – identifying the right media opportunities to reach the target audience and fulfil the brief.

■ Media buying – choosing specific media to get the most impact within the client's budget.

■ Creative – putting advertising ideas into effective words and images to communicate with the target market.

> 'When people aren't having any fun they seldom produce good advertising.'
>
> David Ogilvy (Ogilvy (1978))

Direct sales

■ Account management – as before, acting as the interface between the client and the agency, and leading the agency team in their activities.

■ Database management – developing and maintaining records to provide information on such things as individual customers, prospects, and buying patterns, which can be analysed to inform future strategy.

> 'A good salesman has two ears and one mouth and uses them in that proportion.'
>
> Andi Robertson

■ Channel planning – using data to identify the best way to implement direct marketing.

■ Production/creative – putting the direct marketing plan into action.

Market research

■ Research planning – planning and co-ordinating the collection, analysis and interpretation of data, which may be collected through surveys, questionnaires, interviews or focus groups.

■ Interviewing – conducting interviews face-to-face, by telephone or through focus groups. This may involve recording the results on paper, on a computer or using audio or visual recordings. The interviewees may be specific groups of consumers, businesses, or members of the general public.

■ Secret shopper – buying products, using services or interacting with organisations to find out how they are presenting themselves to their customers.

CHANGING CONDITIONS, NEW ACTIVITIES

The number of people working in the marketing sector has steadily increased. For comparison, there are now more marketers than teachers in the UK.

The biggest spenders on marketing activity in 2008 were hotels and catering, charities and the food industry. But in the constantly changing economic conditions, it is difficulty to predict the sectors that will lead in the future.

Marketing activities both reflect and are influenced by the business environment. The 'challenging' state of the economy in 2009 could lead to organisations increasing their marketing to make sure they keep a share of their particular market and improve their turnover. Alternatively, some may decide to cut back in order to save costs.

Meanwhile, on-going changes in the scope and emphasis of marketing activity are largely a result of the globalisation of markets, and of our increased access to information via the internet and mobile communications channels. As the IT specialists continually dream up more ways to reach individuals with personalised and targeted messages, the possibilities for marketing increase dramatically.

Here are some examples of more recent developments, but of course particular marketing activities will continually evolve and change in importance.

Internal marketing

This emerging concept, which is also called employer branding, looks at training employees to maintain the brand across their activities to attract and retain customers.

Internet marketing

Continual advances in information technology have led to more sophisticated collection and analysis of data about existing and potential customers. This in turn allows producers/sellers to segment their markets more (multiple smaller groups of customers), and creates a need for ever more specialist marketing skills. For example, new skills in customer relationship management (CRM) and the associated software are often required of professional marketers.

SEO – search engine optimisation

Changes in the way we shop have placed greater importance on the internet as a marketplace for both retail consumers and those in the market for public services. Websites are the stalls in this market, and in case you haven't come across this term, SEO is about making websites more effective at attracting visitors. When you type some key words into Google, for example, sophisticated systems search across the whole internet for matches. They are sorted and ranked, and this is what controls the sites that appear in your results.

Positioning is an absolutely critical component of the marketing mix. When the customer is ready to buy, whoever is in that place at that time wins the sale. So you must first be positioned in the place where your customer is – in his list of possible websites. And secondly you need to be in a better position than your competitors – higher up the list. Research has shown that approximately 70% of users, if they click, will click on one the first three listings in a search engine.

All bosses should want potential customers to find his or her company near the top of the list, and so website designers continually try to include the triggers that search engines looks for. Today, search engine optimisation is a key marketing strategy for many organisations, creating demand for marketing skills in this area. The growth of SEO has proved so successful that business spend in the sector continues to increase, and opens up further opportunities for specialist marketers.

Email marketing

The 21st century take on direct mail is email marketing. Instead of mail dropping through your letter box you get emails in your inbox. As with the paper version, marketers strive to make sure their message is read and acted upon.

Pay-per-click

Following on the heels of search engine optimisation and email campaigns, methods of measuring effectiveness (response rates) become important. And closely following this is a new way of advertising: pay-per-click. You are charged for your marketing message or e-advert on the number of responses received – 'clicks' on the link to a website that it contains. Of course this can be the clearest indication of how successful the message was, and equates to ticking the box for 'where did you hear about this product?' when the consumer responds on paper or over the phone.

'Mobile' marketing

As more of us use ever more sophisticated mobile communications, a marketer's dream of personalising their message and targeting it to carefully selected market segments comes closer. It is sometimes called personalised marketing or one-to-one marketing. The possibility of sending messages to mobile phones opens many opportunities. For example, specific advertising messages could be triggered as potential customers enter a shopping mall. The demand for expertise in these areas grows with the possibilities.

Today's aspiring marketer needs an understanding of traditional and current possibilities, and among the most successful will be those who develop new marketing methods for the future.

If the size of the company is sufficiently large, employees may specialise in one of these areas; however in small companies generalists prevail so some may find that they are required to fulfil different roles as and when the need arises.

HOW MUCH DO THEY GET PAID?

The highest rates of pay are found in London and the southeast, where many corporate HQs are located, with the lowest in the northeast and Northern Ireland where they are 8% lower.

So, what might you expect to earn as a marketing professional in 2008–9, compared to other comparable occupations such as finance, IT, HR and sales?

Basic salary comparison

job title	marketing	others (average)
Head of Department	55,000	54,364
Senior Manager	42,000	43,991
Middle Manager	33,500	35,687
Junior Manager	27,000	29,265
Graduate Supervisor	22,000	23,959

Source: Extracted from *Marketing Rewards* published by Croner Reward in association with The Chartered Institute of Marketing.

Don't forget that bonuses could make all the difference to the figures. Bonus payments are often made to marketing personnel. In 2008 38% of directors received 18% of basic pay as a bonus, whereas the average graduate supervisor who received a bonus got 3%. However, nearly a third of directors reported working more than 50 hours a week.

Of course, in some marketing disciplines the bonus level is considerably higher. In sales, for instance, up to 50% of the package is made up of bonus payments.

As with other professions, some companies provide other benefits such as private health insurance (around 50%), and 75% have a company pension scheme.

The MSSSB reports that the pay gap has widened at all levels of seniority apart from middle managers, where it still exists but is narrower than the previous year. However, these statistics must be considered against those for the workforce in general. According to the Office of National Statistics (ONS), the gender pay gap was 17.4% in 1997 and narrowed to 12.8% in 2008. The smallest mean gender pay gap is for 'Sales and customer service occupations' (8.4%) and the widest is for 'Managers and senior officials' (26.6%).

IS IT WORTH IT?

Job satisfaction is high among marketers – 90% rated it as fair, good or excellent – and 92% feel they have fair to excellent job security.

And they feel justly rewarded too: 89% believe their pay is equal to or above market rates and 72% feel they have promotion prospects in their current company.

In this chapter we have explored the roles that are waiting to be filled by those who want to become part of the growing marketing industry, and checked on the kind of rewards they will bring. Now we need to look at how some of the activities are actually performed, so that you will get a feel for what you may be doing if you enter this brave new world.

Let's now look at the sort of thing a marketer might get up to during his (or her) working week through the eyes of one of your potential colleagues, Ben.

Chapter Three

WHAT DOES MARKETING WORK REALLY INVOLVE?

In this chapter I'll show you some of the tools you might use during the course of your work, to give you an idea of what you might get up to on a day-to-day basis if you choose marketing as a career. Things like research, focus groups, the marketing plan, press releases and advertising.

We will use the 'Widget': that famous mythical product or service that has no substance, no meaning as the basis for this illustration. It is defined as an unnamed, unspecified, or hypothetical manufactured good or product.

Let's assume that Ben is a young marketer, new to a company which has a small marketing department. His boss marches into the office one day and gives him his big break. He asks for marketing support in the design and manufacture of the company's new baby, the Widget; the wonderful Widget – the company's recession busting product. Not only that, but Ben's boss also asks him for ideas on how best to launch the Widget. Let's consider what his involvement might consist of as the Widget is designed, manufactured and then hits the shelves. This is a small company, so Ben in many respects is the marketing team. In large companies there will often be a specific research department to handle this but in Ben's case he is required by necessity to be a generalist.

> 'The beginning is the most important part of the work.'
>
> Plato

This is quite common. We'll see some of what Ben has to do to ensure that the launch of the Widget will work for him and his career, not to mention the company and its profit margin.

LOOKING BEFORE YOU LEAP – MARKET RESEARCH

Perhaps one of the most important things that Ben needs to consider in the early stages of the Widget's life is the matter of research. It is not surprising that he is probably keen to get on with it, but it is essential to inform the design and manufacture process by conducting research, and this will be the first thing Ben's boss will be expecting him to look at. Ben knows it will be worth it in the long run. Frequently, taking the time to 'look before you leap' has uncovered time-consuming and costly issues that could otherwise have killed off a product like the Widget in its infancy.

Research should be a cost effective way of finding out what people believe, think, want, need or do. Ben can find these things out by reading research that has already been done (known as secondary research) or by doing the research himself (known as primary research). What he finds out will help the Widget throughout its life cycle, from design to launch and beyond. Let's look at these areas in a little more detail.

There may be a variety of places where he can go and look for this information and some are listed below. Ben should take time out to do some secondary research and explore which ones would be most relevant at each stage of the Widget's development.

Associations – most industries have associations to represent them like the Chartered Institute of Marketing (CIM) and the Law Society of the General Medical Council (GMC). They provide advice and support to members.

Magazines – there are more trade industry-specific journals and newspapers and magazines being published now than ever before, so there may well be one such magazine dedicated to the Widget's marketplace.

Local and National Government – eg the Office of National Statistics provides free data and information on any activity undertaken by a Government department or organisation associated with official channels.

Chambers of commerce – exist to promote local businesses and so may be in a position to be of assistance to marketers, as are other public bodies.

Consumer organisations – such as *Which*? magazine, which champions the consumer and prides itself as being representative of potential and existing customers.

Media – newspapers, TV, radio etc.

Internet – with its astonishing array of information.

Competitors – may help by providing advice.

The library

Ben could therefore do something as basic as visit his local library's reference section (where a wealth of national and regional information is freely available) or check out what has been published in magazines and newspapers about the Widget's marketplace. Inevitably surfing the net will also produce results too. All this information could help those designing, making and then selling the Widget to do a better job.

Ben could also consider primary research, which he does himself. There are many options to choose from, which could include the following.

Focus groups – exploring/recording the beliefs and opinions of a selected group of people, to be better informed about potential customers' needs and inclinations. There is a more detailed section on focus groups later in this chapter.

Questionaires – which are handed or sent out, and the results analysed.

Surveys – which are done by Ben himself with a checklist of things to observe; again the responses are carefully analysed.

Footfall counts – eg recording statistics about customers as they visit a shop.

Interviews – for example a one-to-one visit or a telephone call with potential customers to gather more detailed data.

Product sampling – testing customers' responses and feelings about a prototype of the Widget.

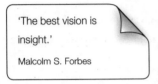

'The best vision is insight.'

Malcolm S. Forbes

In this scenario there are two principal groups of people that Ben should look at carefully: competitors and customers. Gaining a thorough knowledge of both groups will reduce the chances of making a mistake, and increase Ben's chances of helping his colleagues design, create and sell the Widget, and make it a profitable new line for the company. So what questions has Ben noted down about each of these groups?

Some questions about his competitors

Ben's competitors will be good at some things and bad at others. They may have been active in his chosen market for some years, so he may have quite a lot to learn from them. While some of the competition may not be willing to talk or help Ben for obvious reasons, others, perhaps some distance away, may be delighted to help and the knowledge gained from these people could well prove to be invaluable to all those involved in the Widget's life cycle. Ben has decided to ask the following questions.

■ Does anyone else make a similar product or offer a similar service?

■ How much do they sell it for?

■ Where do they sell it?

■ What other products do they sell?

■ What is the standard of quality offered?

■ What are their unique selling points?

Some questions about his customers

Ben must make absolutely sure that he knows what his customers expect, who they are buying from at the moment and why they might prefer to buy the Widget. If Ben can consult his customers from the start of his involvement and throughout the life cycle of the Widget, he can make sure he knows what the expectations and needs of his potential customers are and will improve his chances of creating and then meeting their demands efficiently and profitably. So he plans to ask the following.

- Is there anything potential customers don't like about the Widget?

- Where would they expect to buy the product or service?

- How much would they be prepared to pay?

- Who would they buy this Widget for?

- Where have they bought this product or service in the past?

- What were their likes/dislikes?

Research done by Ben should be very helpful at all stages of the product life cycle and it will also help him deal with areas like product development and pricing.

Let's look at one dynamic and lively method of conducting research that can be informative to all stages of Ben's involvement: the focus group.

A focus group

A focus group consists of anything up to a dozen existing and potential customers or clients who assemble under the watchful eye of the group's leader. The *raison d'être* of a focus group is to provide a focus of opinion and source of ideas. The members of the focus group therefore participate in sessions to provide feedback and give their opinions. These reactions are noted down by the group leader and may then be taken into consideration by the Widget's design team, or could be used by Ben to help him choose where to advertise and to reach his target customer base when promoting the Widget.

Ben has noted down some rules to abide by when he is running his focus group. Here they are.

- The group leader must ask relevant questions to ensure that the data collected produces information that will benefit the research objectives.

■   The group must try to be objective and be honest.

■   The group leader is not a participant; his or her job is to run the
    meeting, explain why they are there and what they are trying to
    achieve, and ensure that the group stays on track. It is best for the
    leader to sit on the edge or the group and observe what happens,
    taking notes for later discussion, and it is imperative that he or
    she resists the temptation to argue with the participants when the
    discussion becomes critical!

■   Non-verbal responses should be observed and a record made.
    These sessions are often videoed and each participant's notes and
    jottings retained.

Remember, you don't want your ideas falling into the wrong hands, so
take advice and use a confidentiality agreement if you need to.

Ben decides to have a colleague chair the group and deal with the nuts
and bolts of running the session, while he acts as an observer only,
recording reactions and views as accurately as possible.

Brainstorming is another activity Ben can use in a focus group. It is used
a great deal by advertising agencies to elicit imaginative advertising ideas
from their employees, and Ben plans to use one particular brainstorming
device to find a name for the Widget. He intends to get the group to
close their eyes and then he will read out clearly 12 pre-prepared words
that illustrate the values of the Widget (quality, user friendly, cutting edge,
reliability etc.). On opening their eyes he'll get the group to write the first
product name that come into their head. Then he is going to note each
person's idea on a flip chart for all to see and to discuss. He has done
this before and was amazed at both the group's enthusiasm and the
results!

As usual there are rules that should be followed for successful focus
groups. Objectivity, good analysis, observation and efficient evaluation
will all contribute to the successful gathering of accurate information.
Ben doesn't forget that good data means that he will be well informed
about his potential customers' needs, and this in turn means that he'll
have a better chance of successfully supporting other departments and
launching his Widget.

Collating your research

The focus group is just one of many research techniques that can be employed to increase the chances of our marketer contributing to the creation and successful launch of the Widget.

Ben will, of course, have the task of analysing the information on customers, competitors and suppliers that he has collected. He then has the task of applying the findings of this work to the relevant design, manufacturing or promotional stages of his marketing work.

It would also be a good idea for Ben to ask himself some questions about his research to make sure that he has some valid data.

■ Is the research informative, interesting and to the point? Does it address the question that you want answered?

■ Are the writers unbiased? What were their reasons for writing what they did?

■ Do primary research/secondary research make any assumptions? Are these assumptions justifiable and appropriate?

■ Are the aims of any research you use or do yourself, clear, concise and precise?

■ Are you happy that the research method and choice of participants is ethically sound?

■ Does the analysis and conclusion make sense and is it relevant?

■ Is the research and conclusion drawn understandable?

Other questions need to be asked about the method of research as well as samples and data collected.

This evaluation process is best thought through at the outset if it is to be of practical use. For instance, if Ben had decided to use a questionnaire or a survey to find out what his potential customers thought about the prototype Widget, he would be well advised to consider how he was going to process the information that the questionnaire has produced. There is software that will do this for you (at a price) but in Ben's case he would probably have to do it manually. He will need to communicate the results of his research in graphic form and this is best done by using pie charts and the like. So, if the statistics resulting from research cannot easily be converted into graphics, there's no point collecting them in the first place.

BEN'S MARKETING CAMPAIGN

Let's assume the Widget has been designed and manufactured; how are we going to sell it?

Ben knows that the best way to produce an effective marketing campaign is to use one or more of the following main promotional methods.

Direct response – is a marketing technique that can use all general advertising media, such as print and electronic, but generally refers to direct mail and telemarketing.

Direct mail – posted communication that has low results (often below 1% response) but has the distinct advantage of being cheap.

Telephone marketing – the act of selling, soliciting or promoting a product or service over the telephone. The ubiquitous telephone sales call can now come from all parts of the globe and shows no sign of being abandoned by companies who need to communicate quickly and cheaply with customers.

Email marketing – campaigns in which stand alone advertisements are sent by email to a targeted list of recipients. Internet marketing has many forms, including advertising, paid and unpaid, newsletters, blogs etc. (The use of the internet and email is the most rapidly growing form of marketing communication).

Direct sales – face-to-face contact, often on a one-to-one basis, is still much used today, especially where complex subjects such as buying a car or financial services products are concerned.

Public relations – concerns the management of the information flow between an organisation and its public. The use of PR specialists provides an individual or company with exposure to an audience using topics of public interest and news items.

Strategic alliances – involve entering into significant long-term partnership and collaborative agreements between two companies that can gain advantages for both using complementary campaigns, cross-promotions, and data exchange.

Once Ben has chosen the right combination of the methods noted above, he will be asked to explain his conclusions to his boss.

So how does he present his ideas to his boss and his colleagues?

Ben has already thought about this and he collates his ideas in the marketing plan format that will be expected using the standard headings below, this will then be circulated to management and discussed at a meeting.

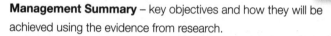

Ben's marketing plan outline

Management Summary – key objectives and how they will be achieved using the evidence from research.

Product Market Situation – description of the market Ben intends to operate in, including reference to current trends, customer profiles and pricing.

SWOT analysis – identifying the internal (strengths, weaknesses) and external (opportunities and threats) factors affecting both the company and the product that will help or hinder achieving an objective.

Marketing Objectives – marketing goals should always be SMART: Specific, Measurable, Realistic and within a sensible Timescale.

Marketing Strategies – Ben will describe how and where the product is going to be distributed and sold.

Action Programme – specific action points that define who does what and when.

Budget – the costs of implementing Ben's marketing campaign, listed in detail, and their impact on potential profitability through sales. Sometimes called a cost/benefit analysis.

Control and Evaluation – Ben establishes who is in charge of the various stages of the campaign and defines 'success', eg the number of Widgets sold.

Contingencies – anything relevant but not covered above.

Events

The event is used as both a sales and PR tool and those of us who have spent any time in the marketing world will have probably been to more events then we care to remember. They are frequently used to launch new products, rebrand products (such as Jif to Cif) and companies (for instance the arrival of the new giants of the financial world Aviva, the new name for Norwich Union), new sales campaigns, conferences, and also to celebrate the achievement of departments or individuals.

In short, a well planned event is a vital part of the marketer's toolbox.

The choice of venue for the Widget's launch is crucial. Ben needs to be sure that his choice will suit the occasion, and as he plans his launch he makes notes creating a checklist to help him and those who are working with him. His checklist include references to food, pre-event publicity (PR and press releases), invitations, seating, treatment of VIPs, parking, photographers, records of attendance and paperwork such as registration. This list is not exhaustive and Ben must ensure that he has contingency planning in place for unexpected developments; he must also check all the equipment he is going to use and ensure that everyone is briefed sufficiently.

Events are nearly always harder work then you imagined, but they often bring rewards unobtainable elsewhere; you can always relax when it's all over!

Ben's press release

Now Ben must think about communicating with his potential customers. The press release is sent to all types of press and media. Press releases are often used by public relation companies and departments, but they are also used by other marketing professionals and certainly may be usefully employed as part of a marketing campaign, as we have seen. In a small firm you may have to do your own PR.

The business information company Cobweb describes a press release as being 'a simplified story about your company or a particular aspect of it, written from a news point of view'. Press releases are written when you have a newsworthy subject to write about, such as the launch of a new product, a change of image or a forthcoming event.

Fortunately, Ben is a dab hand at press releases and he knows the rules.

Press release basics

- You should give each release a headline; it's not necessary for it to be witty because the journalist will probably want to invent a title of their own.

- Do some research, talk to the journalist or editor and find out what sort of material they are looking for.

- NEWS RELEASE or PRESS RELEASE should be written clearly at the top of the page.

- Use headed paper and put your name, address and contact details at the end.

- Double space your text so that the recipient can edit it.

- Keep it short and simple (KISS), using one side of A4 where possible, and restricting the text to three main points.

- Try to use quotations to enliven the message.

- Only delay (embargo) the publication if you have to.

- When you come to the end write 'end'. If you need to use a second page write 'continued' at the foot of the page.

- Avoid jargon and flowery language, and don't be too technical.

Ben sends his press release to the chosen media company in the hope that the editor or journalist will use it as the basis for an article or programme. This achieves two things: he gets his publicity, and the media company gets a story to tell. As you can see this is a mutually beneficial arrangement and it is free.

'Kodak sells film, but they don't advertise film. They advertise memories.'

Theodore Parker

Advertising

Ben knows there are some important considerations to bear in mind when choosing what form of advertising he wishes to use to promote the Widget.

Ben must ensure that anything he does fits with the company's over-arching marketing and branding strategy. He knew it wasn't going to be a picnic, and he was right! Obviously advertising can be used for other purposes, for example brand promotion.

Brand advertising is used by all sorts of companies, large and small. Coca-Cola, for instance, have an internationally accepted brand and the large car manufacturers are continually trying to build and increase awareness of their brand. It is expensive and is only really effective once a company is well established. Ben soon realises that this is not really what he was looking for.

What Ben wants in this example is direct response advertising. It has a far wider application, and is characterised by four primary elements.

- Offer – the product or a benefit it can bestow is shown or described. For example, a luxury car may be offered as a status symbol, giving you not only comfort and performance, but also prestige and admiration.

- Information – enough to encourage the consumer to make a decision to take up the offer and find out more (what it can do, and perhaps how much it costs).

- A call to action – a direct instruction or a suggestion for what the potential customer should do. 'Call today to realise your dreams!' 'Click here for the finest Widgets!'

■ The way to respond – such as any or all of: a free number, an address, a web page, an email address.

The purpose of direct response advertising is, as the name suggests, to produce a clear and measurable response. The type of response varies depending on the kind of business and overall marketing strategy involved. He must try to ensure that the response of customers is measurable. If it works he can run the ad again, if it doesn't he can change it or scrap it altogether.

Advertising at its best

In 2004 Ogilvy & Mather launched a campaign for Dove that became a world-wide success story and won them an International Advertiser of the year award in 2005.

The strength of the campaign was in its universal single idea that works in any country, the 'campaign for real beauty'. They had come up with the concept in 2003 for a campaign that used different sized 'real' women rather than the normal stick-thin models who appear in beauty product adverts. The follow-up campaign was photographed and designed using models from each geographical and cultural area where the ads would appear.

The adverts appeared on buildings, poster sites and train stations in every major city. It was backed up by a field marketing exercise, collecting 800,000 responses in eight days. People were also able to telephone in responses, and 500,000 had responded within a week.

This massive and innovative campaign was hugely successful, not least because it generated free media coverage in newspapers and on the most popular day time television shows. It has been worked out that the media coverage generated was worth 30 times more than the paid-for media space.

All this helped increase sales in the US by 13%. Primary tests conducted in six department stores showed that sales of Dove products increased by 163% over the first month that the campaign ran. A month later the tests showed that sales had increased by 135%. By the end of 2005, Dove's market share in the Asia-Pacific region had increased from 19% to 26%.

This marketing campaign included advertisements, video, workshops, sleepover events and even the publication of a book and the production of a play. As a follow-up, in an effort to promote a newly established 'Self-Esteem Fund', Dove ordered a series of highly-successful online-based short films promoting the self-esteem concept.

There is a classic formula used by advertisers and Ben's company uses it all the time. It's well worth remembering. The formula is AIDA, which stands for:

- Attention – the most important thing an ad must do is grab the reader's attention. You can do this with a great headline and good design of the advert.

- Interest – once you've got their attention, you need to arouse their interest in your product or service.

- Desire – you need to convert the interest into desire for what you are offering. Interest doesn't lead to a sale.

- Action – even if the reader desires your product, it's not enough – you want them to take action. Put a call to action at the end of the ad; tell the reader what to do to next, and make it easy for them to do it. Even if you have a great ad, it's wasted if you don't tell people exactly how to take action.

AIDA – an example

One of my past bosses was a great exponent of AIDA. He was an ex-barrow boy who had soared to dizzy heights in the company's hierarchy. It was impossible to ignore this man; he always grabbed your attention and often managed to lace his presentations with a great sense of humour.

I once encountered him as I wandered about at a conference, munching M&Ms and saying hi to people. He was gazing glumly into his drink.

'What's wrong?' I asked.

'In about ten minutes' he replied, 'I have to give the "keynote" speech at this evening's climatic rah-rah session at the end of the conference, and I haven't got a clue what to say.'

I didn't know what to say either, so I offered him an M&M chocolate. Absentmindedly, he took one and then suddenly started staring at it with a 'eureka' expression on his face.

He snatched the packet out of my hand and abruptly asked the bartender if he had any more.

'Yeah, sure,' the barman said.

'I'll have the lot!' my boss cried. 'I'll have every M&M you have in this hotel!' He smiled at me, 'That's it – it's sorted,' and marched off.

Not long after some three hundred of us sat expectantly in the conference hall. The hum of expectation died as my boss was introduced. He marched down towards the central stage under a bright spotlight and began throwing M&Ms at the audience shouting 'M and M'. He climbed on to the stage and continued with the barrage.

Someone got a sore eye from one of the packs of airborne chocolates and other packets burst open on impact. My boss was soon striding across the stage, wise-cracking with friends in the audience.

Laughter filled the hall but eventually the mayhem subsided as the boxes emptied. A silence descended and my boss walked to the front of the stage and shouted 'What does M&M mean?'

A variety of answers were shouted back – some not entirely appropriate or decent.

'I'll tell you,' he said eventually, and then went on to give the best speech of the conference on two of his favourite sales techniques: 'Marking up' (or offering an up market higher price option) and 'Multi-selling' (offering other products and services) at every sale.

He completed his presentation by explaining the benefits to customer and staff of following his advice and outlining how these suggestions could be built into day-to-day activity. It was all very clear and positive.

He got a standing ovation, not necessarily for the quality of the speech, but because he had made us laugh and above all this great exponent of AIDA had grabbed our attention the moment he first appeared in the hall!

Well there we are. Ben has shown us a little of what you might get up to if you become a marketer; he has done some research and we have looked in detail at one of his chosen methods of finding out what his customers think: the focus group.

He has considered some promotional methods and we have seen him preparing to write a marketing plan for his boss.

We have examined two tools that he plans to use for the launch, namely a press release and advertising. We shall leave him as he prepares to launch the Widget.

Many other marketing tools exist to help Ben, the budding marketer, to achieve his objectives, and his choices in this chapter could have been different. This isn't an exhaustive description of a marketing campaign, merely an attempt to introduce you to some of the things you might get involved in. Was the Widget launched successfully? We will never know, because of course it doesn't exist, but when your boss strolls in and hands you your first big break, remember Ben – it might come in handy!

Chapter Four
SKILLS AND ATTRIBUTES – IS MARKETING RIGHT FOR ME?

As we have already discovered, the discipline of 'marketing' covers a very wide range of activities. Not only that, but almost every organisation – private, public, wholesale, retail or not-for-profit – can use the services of a marketer. Marketing can be performed by a specialised agency or consultant, or it can be kept in house. And of course, the point is frequently made that every member of staff can become involved in marketing because it is like a thread that runs throughout the activities of organisations.

SO HOW AND WHERE DOES A PROSPECTIVE MARKETER BEGIN?

You need to begin with yourself, by assessing your aptitudes, interests and skills. Almost any combination will be suitable for some part of the marketing function. And if you have several areas covered, then you could be a very valuable member of a marketing team.

Before marketing became quite so diverse, it was often said that a marketing specialist would need to be able to use both the left side (scientific) and the right side (creative) of their brain. They would need to collect and analyse data, as well as think creatively to produce campaigns. Now, because the marketing function is expanding into new directions and techniques, you may have the opportunity to specialise in one particular area more effectively. But you will progress better in your career if you have a wider range of skills and, more importantly, can appreciate the business context you operate in.

> 'The best thing about the future is that it only comes one day at a time.'
>
> Abraham Lincoln

When you have honestly assessed what you are good at and what you enjoy, you will need to look at your qualifications, and decide if you are prepared to study further. Your academic qualifications will determine your entry level into the profession, and probably your potential career development.

> 'Ability is what you're capable of doing. Motivation determines what you do. Attitude determines how well you do it.'
>
> Lou Holtz

Where do you want to end up? If you want to climb the career ladder, you will need to consider how you will gain the skills, qualifications and experience to reach each rung.

Who am I? Who could I be?

What do you like/dislike about your work or study?

Who is your working hero, what do they do?

Write down all the things you are passionate about. How could they fit into your career?

How quiet or are you outgoing? What sort of job requires you to be like that?

Look at yourself through the eyes of an employer. Do a SWOT analysis on yourself to identify your personal strengths and weaknesses in terms of your personality, qualifications and skills, and the opportunities and threats that exist in the marketplace for the kind of job you are looking for.

Consider how you define success. Do you feel you're successful in what you do? If not, why not?

Ask yourself the magic question: 'What kind of activities would my ideal job involve?'

FIRST THINGS FIRST

What are you good at, and what do you like doing? Is your brain left (scientific) or right (creative) dominant? And does this matter? Or do you really need both to be a successful marketer?

We need to put aside the old ideas that marketing is only about communication and promotional activity (although of course they are important), or that it is solely based on behavioural science, referring to sales methods established decades ago.

We can look at three distinct strands of marketing activity to follow: scientific/numerical/technological, creative, and humanities.

Science and technology

Our life cycle model (Chapter One) shows that the process begins with research and design, to produce and test a product. The prototype, which could of course be a service, is then tested in the marketplace (see Chapter Four on 'tools'), where market research will feed back into the final design. For this area of work your skills need to be numeric, to create meaningful data and statistical analysis.

Statistics

The information gathered will also be used by the marketer to direct other areas of their campaign. Market research helps identify typical customer groups, and allows market segmentation, which means that advertising and promotional activity can be tailored in content and style to appeal to a specific consumer.

Marketing metrics

It has often been said that companies waste half the money they spend on advertising, but the problem is knowing which half is successful. Research into the effects of marketing activity is continuous for many products and services, to make sure that resources are targeted in the most productive and cost-effective ways. What produced an increase in awareness or sales? Which customers responded to which campaigns? What were the costs and benefits? Careful selection of the metrics used, and analysis and interpretation of the statistical data gathered, is a specialism of its own.

With increasingly sophisticated methods of measurement in our digital age, identifying the successful activities is becoming an important focus. Marketers in all disciplines must be able to test and measure in a scientific manner; quantifiable benefits must be demonstrated, and the return on investment must be clear.

IT

Marketing has changed dramatically with the rise and rise of our reliance on the internet and email for information gathering and for buying goods and services. Now there are many ways to use IT skills in this area, and the opportunities change and increase along with the technology. You can really combine creative thinking with technological knowledge to market in innovative ways.

A few examples are given below.

Search engine optimisation (SEO) has become crucial for any enterprise that uses a website as part of its marketing mix. By understanding and capitalising on the ways in which search engines work, a skilled operator can ensure that a website rises to the first page of listings without paying for the privilege. This is the modern equivalent of taking advertising space in carefully targeted print media a few years ago.

Direct mail is still widely used, but email is taking over. Being able to make full use of the software available for CRM (customer relationship management) is another highly desirable skill in marketing today.

The new kid on the block is text marketing – with spin offs for location-specific messages.

Creative

This is where the 'traditional' view of marketing still holds good. A rounded marketing campaign still includes all the elements of creativity that it always has: innovation, clever words, and good design.

The physical design of a product that make it do its job efficiently, and the aesthetics that make it appealing to consumers, are extremely important. And it is similar for services. Optimising the design to attract more sales, or make sales to different markets, is a challenge that can be tackled with the use of market research information, but the data has to be interpreted and executed by creative talent.

Information about this wonderful, attractive product must be communicated to the waiting, potential consumers. And here creativity is key. Branding must be established. Each press release must be carefully crafted in the right language. Each advert must have great visual elements and wording. Events must be dreamed up to attract attention, guerrilla marketing might be employed and websites developed to be eye-catching. The possibilities are as numerous as the ideas a creative person can come up with.

> 'Products are made in the factory, but brands are created in the mind.'
>
> Walter Landor

Humanities

Is your skill base more people related? Is your interest aroused by what makes people tick, and how they interact? Is what you do directed by your moral and ethical stance? How important is public service to you? Is there a particular cause that is dear to your heart? Do you want to help 'save the world'?

Some fundamental questions; and the answers you give might appear to steer you away from the apparently commercial, profit-motivated world of marketing. But let's look at this more closely. There are two distinct strands to consider.

Psychology/behavioural science

Marketing is largely about influencing people's behaviour. If you're selling widgets you want to influence as many people as possible to buy them.

And as we have seen, you do this by making the most attractive widgets you can, raising awareness of widgets in general and the attributes of your particular widgets, persuading people to buy them and then keeping your customers happy so that they will buy more and recommend them (and you) to their friends.

For example, the use of herd behaviour in marketing uses the idea that people will buy more of products that are seen to be popular. This idea is appealing to supermarkets because it offers the opportunity to increase sales without the need to give people discounts.

The ways in which our marketing methods work – focus groups, advertising, events or whatever – is understood by behavioural scientists. This area of expertise is a small but important part of the marketing mix, helping the marketer to understand how individuals and groups respond, and helping to predict the results of the elements of a marketing campaign.

Social sciences

Marketing is informed and influenced by many of the social sciences, particularly psychology, sociology, and economics. Anthropology is also a small, but growing influence. So entry into a marketing career can begin with training in a wide variety of disciplines.

All the skills we have talked about so far are just as applicable to public goods (provided by the Government for the benefit of us all) and charities as they are to selling gifts for Christmas. As well as consumer goods and services, marketing is an integral part of industry, construction, financial goods and services, tourism, not-for-profit organisations and the public sector.

> 'Choose a job you love, and you will never have to work a day in your life.'
>
> Confucius

And there's more…

However, it's not quite as simple as recognising your innate skills and interests. Once you have decided your general area of aptitude, there is a growing expectation that marketers of all disciplines will have a wider awareness of the commercial environment that they are part of. Business skills and experience enable the marketer to target their primary skills towards the bottom line (and this applies to social and cause-related marketing just as much). In terms of career advancement and promotion to management levels, then business acumen or entrepreneurship will be very important. And if you rise to management levels, you certainly can't expect to direct the work of others with different skills if you don't have a good understanding of what they do.

ARE YOU A MARKETER?

What marketing role you choose to have is up to you. You could be anything from a researcher to an advertising executive. You are limited only by how much energy and determination you use. A grasp of figures and English is useful, but many people have overcome all sorts of personal barriers to become successful marketers. It's important at the outset to try to see if a people business like marketing suits you.

Not everyone is cut out for life in marketing and brand management. Succeeding in the field requires a very specific set of personality traits. See how well you match up.

Enthusiasm

A fascination with the marketing process will give you the drive that will make you a great marketer.

Leadership

A brand manager must be able to develop a strategy and then champion it and communicate it. You must be able to get people to work together towards a common goal and achieve results.

Creativity

To make your products stand out in a crowded market, a brand manager must create and develop ideas. You must be able to 'think outside the box' and develop your sense of humour.

Good communication

A brand manager must be good with words, both spoken and written, to lead meetings and write project proposals that will be reviewed by senior management. Clear, analytical, and persuasive writing and presentation skills are vital.

Teamwork

Teamwork is the most essential skill in marketing. Most work is done in teams so you must be able to encourage and participate in effective teamwork. Looking further ahead, more senior roles will also involve managing people. You will need to learn how to train, mentor, and motivate people.

Analytical

A brand manager must work to achieve business objectives, and so need to be able to track progress and understand how to grow market share and volume.

Adaptability

The marketing environment is always changing. You will typically only be assigned to any brand for 12 to 18 months, and they may be totally different. One week you may be promoting the charms of widgets, the following one enthusing about chewing gum. You will have to be able to adapt quickly and have make a difference from the start.

Risk taking

Every day new products are introduced in strategic ways that force established brands to 'reinvent' themselves, or at least rethink their marketing programmes. A brand manager must be able to look at business situations from a variety of perspectives and take acceptable risks. You must feel comfortable making smart business decisions when not all the data is available and when using your intuition is crucial.

Good judgement

Marketing professionals must not be swayed by personal biases. For instance, even if you think a particular ad campaign is the best you have ever done, if the consumers in your focus groups hate it you have to put your preference aside.

Try doing the quiz below, and check your answers with the scores at the end.

QUIZ

1 How would you feel if you had to work late?
- ☐ a OK, I want to give 110% to the job.
- ☐ b Only if I had to.
- ☐ c No way, I would only want to work within the hours of my contract.

2 How well do you get on with people in authority eg your boss?
- ☐ a Not very well, I think I could do better.
- ☐ b I get on well with people and would want to work as a team.
- ☐ c I rely on others totally to tell me what to do.

3 Are you tidy when working?
- ☐ a Yes, everything is in its place.
- ☐ b Sometimes, but things can go missing.
- ☐ c No, I don't even think about it.

4 How do you prioritise your work?
- ☐ a Prepare a daily schedule and work to it.
- ☐ b List important tasks and remember the rest.
- ☐ c Deal with issues as and when.

5 How do you cope with several tasks at once?
- ☐ a I deal with the important ones first.
- ☐ b Select the one that interests me first.
- ☐ c Make several starts on various tasks and continue with the easiest one.

6 How do you cope with unexpected problems?
- ☐ a Carefully and systematically.
- ☐ b Use my experience with similar problems in the past.
- ☐ c I am no good at dealing with unexpected difficulties and try to pass them to someone else.

7 Are you a team member?

☐ a No, I work better on my own.

☐ b Sometimes, but I can work on my own if necessary.

☐ c Yes, I enjoy team sports and like to work with others.

8 Do you like your work colleagues/school friends/teachers/ lecturers?

☐ a I tolerate them but keep myself to myself.

☐ b Yes, but I keep a distance while remaining friendly.

☐ c Very much, I enjoy the camaraderie.

9 What do you think about delegation?

☐ a I think it is 'passing the buck' and I would do it myself.

☐ b Sometimes it's a necessary process, particularly if I am to learn more.

☐ c I think it's very useful to pass on a task if you can't do it yourself.

Score

a = 1, b = 2, c = 3.

✅ Your marketing score

9–14 You might be suited to marketing as you like to work independently and are good at getting motivated. But beware, you could overwork yourself and must make sure you plan your free time. Do not become isolated, so you will need to keep in touch with contacts and colleagues – keep networking.

15–22 Your balanced attitude should make you suited to marketing, but you must plan your working life carefully and remember to prioritise.

23–27 You enjoy the company of work colleagues and should consider carefully whether marketing is for you. You will have to develop strict self-discipline to get motivated. If you do decide to become a marketer, make sure you build a strong network of colleagues.

WHAT WOULD I ACTUALLY DO?

Let's look at some examples. These are drawn from the experiences of your author and my collaborator. This is how we really dealt with different parts of marketing campaigns, which I hope will give you an idea of what day-to-day life might be like if you decide to take on a marketing role and help you decide if you would enjoy it.

Look at these notes taken from the actual diary of a marketer, and read about a week in their working life.

A week in the life of a brand manager

Monday

Monday morning always starts with checking the latest brand and product performance charts for any dramatic changes that may need urgent attention.

Assuming all is well, as it seems today, I began checking the status of projects and noticed I needed to chase the creative agency for an update on the latest design.

The afternoon consisted of an internal presentation to the rest of the marketing team on the latest advertising campaign successes and learnings.

Tuesday

Started with a management meeting. This meeting provides us with all the key business information which may affect our marketing and communications plans over the coming months. It also gives me the opportunity to feedback on budget management, variances, and brand performance, and to gain input on the various projects I am managing.

The end of the day was a conference call into Munich. We are running a research development project for a new product we plan to launch in 12 months time. This launch currently depends on the success of the trials the team are running.

I then went on to finalise my presentation for the design agencies the following morning.

Wednesday

The design agency came in this morning for their quarterly update. I presented the latest brand and product performance.

Before I know it we are into the afternoon, and our PR executive has scheduled a meeting to discuss the latest communications update while I provide the latest brand overview and campaign review.

Thursday

We received the latest research back from our London agency. The rest of the day involved dissecting the market research, pulling out the key market insights, and creating a presentation ready for the weekly marketing meeting.

Friday

I reviewed the latest copy for our company magazine. Internal marketing is a key role and important to the success of the product. Once approved I forwarded it to our internal editor for inclusion.

The marketing meeting was cancelled today due to an urgency in another brand team, which left me to answer emails before lunch.

Friday is team lunch day and gives us all a chance to catch up and take a break (we don't get very many in our hectic days!).

The afternoon involved a budget planning session with the finance department before heading off for a much deserved weekend break!

PROJECTS

Now let's explore the activities of a marketer in a different way. This time by looking at extracts from notes taken during the course of a couple of marketing projects.

The Minister's visit

Excerpt from the diary of a further education college marketing assistant.

1st June

The Principal strolled into our office and casually announced, 'There's a ministerial visit in two and a half weeks, can you find something for him to do for a couple of hours?'

That was it, the sum total of my brief. No clues.

I knew that we would need to extract as much marketing benefit from this as possible. Colleges don't have many Ministers visit, and we had an opportunity to raise our profile through the publicity a good event would generate.

Lunchtime with colleagues got the creative juices flowing and a good idea emerged. Why not have him present a prize?

2nd June

'Eureka!' one full litter bin and chewed pencil later, I came up with the idea of a 'Student of the Year' award.

Phone call from Principal five minutes later asking me to 'pop in with an outline for the visit' first thing tomorrow.

Burning the midnight oil.

3rd June

Went to meeting armed with two sheets of paper:

A proposed agenda for the day of the visit.

A list of benefits to the college of my proposed 'Student of the Year Award'.

The P listened, read my meagre offerings, and started to ask questions.

'How are we going to choose the winner of the competition?'

'What is the prize?'

'What shall we do for lunch?'

Etc, etc, and told me to come back in three days with the answers.

6th June

Planning meeting for Heads of Department.

Ensure transparency – set rules of competition, press releases, panel of judges.

Government will not permit us to publicise the visit until the day before, for security reasons, so embargoed press releases until 12 hours before – only guests can be informed beforehand, and only post event publicity allowed.

The Visit

Parking – hadn't anticipated that another event was on the same day and the car park was full, with no room for 40 guests to our event. Ex-policeman on staff to direct traffic.

Photographer called in sick just hours beforehand – spare from art department.

Arranged for large cheque as a prize, but it was way too big to fit in the photo.

My media contact list came up trumps – 2 newspapers, one radio and a possible TV coverage.

P gave fantastic opening speech.

Minister did his part.

Lessons learnt:

Never forget parking.

Always have a back up for a key role.

The PA's story

An excerpt from the diary of the PA to the MD of a small company which produces First Day Covers for postage stamp issues, and retails them by mail and through a couple of shops, along with collectable stamps.

First Day Covers are made more valuable and collectable by being postmarked (on the first day of issue) in a relevant location, and by being treated in a particular way.

1st Sept

That's the fascinating part of working for a small organisation – you can get your fingers into all sorts of pies, and one of those pies has turned out to be pretty big. I have to arrange an event to launch the Christmas stamp issue this year, both to add value to a restricted number of covers and, of course, to generate some publicity.
My initiation into the world of marketing.

4th Sept

The stamps commemorate 100 years of the Church of England Children's Society. Now, there's a nice big, well-known cathedral here in Canterbury, where our offices are... One hundred years, hmmm.... What about an old mail coach? And a postman in historic costume? Oh, and we could ask some local dignitaries along for the ride!

The stamps are issued in November – better start planning, there are lots of pieces to fit together to make this work.

The rest of September was very hectic as I:

Found a coach and horses then arranged permission to drive around the city centre.

Wrote to the Dean of the Cathedral to request permission to start from the cathedral yard, and invited him to join us for the ride and lunch afterwards.

Found a lunch venue, and invited local dignitaries

Informed and invited the local press, radio and TV.

Contacted the PO to arrange special hand franking of the covers.

Found that the PO can provide a postman for the morning, in appropriate costume. Borrowed a posthorn from a local theatre group.

Arranged for selection of hats and cloaks for those on the coach to look the part.

Got leaflets printed.

Got some volunteers from the younger staff to put on costumes and hand out leaflets around the city during the morning.

Limited edition First Day Covers with 'silk' pictures attached, special 'carried by mail coach' imprint and stamps affixed delivered to PO for franking.

18th Nov

Fine but cold. Thank goodness it didn't rain.

Collected a bag of franked covers and took them to the coach for a quick spin around the cathedral before the guests arrived.

Despatched the staff in their costumes and armed with leaflets to give to bemused shoppers.

Welcomed the guests and introduced them to the Dean over coffee.

Made sure the postman was sitting prominently on top of the coach with his horn, and other guests had hats and cloaks. Great fun riding around.

Still 'on duty' over lunch, making sure that the postman had somewhere to change and that everyone enjoyed themselves.

A long, stressful, but strangely exhilarating day!

25th Nov

The event was deemed a success, and received good local coverage in the media. This will increase awareness of our brand of First Day Covers and increase sales in the shops too.

Top of the list of 'Things to do' for the next time:

Make sure you tell everyone, in simple clear terms, exactly what their part is and how it fits into the plan. Don't assume that anyone knows anything. If you tell them and they already know, they'll feel smug and clever. If they didn't know, you will avert potential disaster by telling them!

And a quick search on the internet reveals that those First Day Covers are still changing hands among collectors some 30 years later, clearly marked with a special imprint that they were carried in a mail coach. A lasting legacy to a first marketing experience!

The café from hell

This is an extract from the diary of a young marketer working as a business advisor for an innovation centre.

Day 1

Interesting meeting today with a couple from Birmingham who decided to move to Cornwall and found their ideal home in a quaint village on the edge of Bodmin Moor. So far so good. The only problem was that the property they bought for themselves also contained a café. They knew nothing about cafés and didn't want to have one. However, it's a going concern and they are lumbered with it, whether they like it or not. They came to me asking for help with marketing to make it profitable.

Day 2

Visited the premises and wondered not just what they had let themselves in for, but what I had let myself in for.

I conquered the desire to run and was shown into the most frightful room furnished with chintz table cloths, net curtains soiled napkins, and a collection of 1970s trolls. The only customer was propped up in the corner reading a newspaper. There were no other signs of life except for the sound of someone clearing their throat in the kitchen.

Day 3

After much debate with the hapless owners, who had no idea what to do with this café, we decided to conduct a survey in the immediate locality to see if their prospective customers wanted to have a place to go for a cup or a bite, and more specifically wanted this café. So after much discussion the survey questionnaire was created and then distributed. It was collected in boxes left at strategic points. We also had a word with some customers on a one to one basis to gather further information. And, a member of staff offered to go on a fact-finding visit to another café, which he said had turned business around overnight. So through a combination of surveys, one to one interviews and observation of a competitor, there emerged a consensus that there was a demand locally to establish a year-round trade, especially after closure of the local pub. So after further consultation with a variety of different people, the owners decided to discard trolls, chintz, old table cloths (big bonfire!) and the source sof the throat clearing noises from the kitchen.

A licence to serve alcohol was acquired, and a brilliant cook with excellent reputation for locally sourced simple food was employed. Special deals were offered for identified local groups eg moor rescue groups and pensioners.

Day 4

Went back to see how things were progressing. I found that trade had improved. New name, new cook, new atmosphere, new profit. Wonderful!

Chapter Five
QUALIFICATIONS AND TRAINING

Which is more important? This is the million dollar question. I recall one individual who had no qualifications but was given a month to prove himself in a large company, but this is a rare opportunity. In most cases you will need qualifications or experience, and still expect to undergo training as you work. Even the top handful of graduates that the most prestigious training schemes take each year are still trainees for several years.

Following the one to one interviews completed for this book it seems to me that marketing was a much more fluid and less regimented discipline 20+ years ago, with fewer academic qualifications and less defined routes offered by professional bodies like the CIM. Because of this more people with none or few recognised qualifications (like myself) became marketing professionals.

However, in the marketing world you are thinking about entering it is less common for people to 'fall into the business' partly because so many more people achieve formal qualifications in their chosen subject. And of course it is much easier for a large company to simply pick the best from universities, thus avoiding some of the time-consuming and costly selection process that would be required for unqualified candidates.

This chapter will guide you through an outline of the steps you will need to take from your first idea of working in marketing, through qualifications, training, accreditation and climbing the career ladder.

QUALIFICATIONS

You may have started your formal education in the wonders of marketing at school or college. Both GCSE and A level Business Studies courses include work on marketing, and this may be where your interest was first aroused.

The next level up may be to NVQ, which you may undertake while working or as a full-time student at college.

Where to go for help

Help with this kind of decision making is available through your school, college, or try your local Connexions Direct. Learn Direct offers information about local, distance learning and on-line courses too (see Resources section for contact details). University courses can be found through UCAS, online or in print, as well as direct from each university.

14–19 Diploma

The new Diploma for 14–19 year olds, introduced in September 2009, offers another route into learning about marketing and is obtainable in three grades: Foundation (equivalent to 5 GCSEs grade D–G), Higher (7 GCSEs A*–C) and Advanced (3.5 A levels). You can use them as stepping stones to further or higher education. The Foundation Diploma in Business, Administration and Finance includes topic areas such as business research and promotion while the Higher and Advanced Diplomas cover more areas, including marketing and sales.

Marketing NVQs

Further education colleges offer the NVQ route. City & Guilds is well established and recognised by employers, and has a long-standing track record in vocational qualifications. NVQs are work related, competency based. There are three qualifications to help develop skills to meet the needs and expectations of employers in the UK and overseas, and to boost your CV so that you might climb a few more rungs up the career ladder. City & Guilds also offer related qualifications in social and market research. The qualification structure is simple and flexible, with a varied list of study units that you can combine to make your own personalised NVQ.

Level 2 NVQ in Marketing

An introduction to working with marketing data, meeting objectives, managing resources, and team working. Two mandatory units, four options. Level 2 is equivalent to 5 GCSEs, or 1 A level.

Level 3 NVQ in Marketing

A broad range of marketing activities aimed at the more experienced candidate who wants to develop and implement marketing strategies, design research projects and advertising campaigns, work up databases and run a challenging portfolio of products and services. Three mandatory units, four options. Level 3 is equivalent to 2+ A levels.

Level 4 NVQ in Marketing

A range of choices based around design and evaluation of marketing plans, communication strategies, managing sales relationships, recruiting staff, developing business plans and leading from the front. Four mandatory units, four optional. Level 4 is equivalent to First Degree level.

Apprenticeships

Apprenticeship schemes allow you to learn while you work, so that you can be paid while you build up knowledge and gain qualifications such as NVQs.

The Marketing and Sales Standards Setting Body (MSSSB) is responsible for the development of apprenticeships in the marketing and sales industries, covering marketing, marketing communications, sales and telesales occupations. The MSSSB works to improve standards in marketing and sales, and to develop a national educational and training framework that supports the professions. National Occupational Standards in social marketing are also being developed.

In England and Wales, there are two types of marketing and marketing communications apprenticeships: a Foundation Modern Apprenticeship, which leads to a level 2 NVQ; and an Advanced Modern Apprenticeship, which is a level 3 qualification. Both levels of apprenticeship are available in marketing, marketing communications, sales and telesales.

At both Foundation and Advanced level, you can work in different capacities such as: event management assistant; market research executive/interviewer; marketing assistant/executive. If you are a marketing manager in a SME (small/medium enterprise) but have no formal qualifications, you may be able to undertake an Advanced level apprenticeship; or as a manager who wants to specialise in sales.

MSSSB recommend that Foundation Modern Apprenticeships take 12–18 months to complete, and two to three years for an Advanced Modern Apprenticeship.

If you are not currently working in marketing and or marketing communications and are interested in applying for an apprenticeship, you have two options:

■ approach an employer and see if they are willing to take you on

■ apply through the Learning and Skills Council (LSC) who will put you in touch with a training provider who will try to match you with an employer.

You can then contact the individual awarding bodies to find out more about the individual qualifications.

A survey in December 2008 showed that the average wage per week for an apprentice was around £170, and in some jobs around £210 per week.

For further information you can go to the marketing and sales products sections of the MSSSB website (see Resources section).

Getting a degree – unlimited choices

If you decide to head off to university in the UK, 14% of degrees include a study of marketing, so there is a huge choice. First you will need to decide if you want to study marketing as a single subject or decide what subjects you would like to combine.

Would business studies give you the more rounded knowledge to progress your career? Or are you interested in a particular commercial or industrial area? In this case you could consider, for example, tourism and marketing, or science and marketing. You may be interested in international marketing. Or perhaps you already know which specialism you are suited to and so will consider, for example, graphic design with marketing, or ICT with marketing. And you may add a MSc in Marketing to a First degree qualification.

There are a huge number of degree course that include marketing, either as the main element or jointly with another subject area, or as an optional course. According to the Chartered Institute of Marketing (CIM), one in seven of all UK degrees have a marketing element. To demonstrate just how widely marketing skills can be applied, a quick scan on the UCAS website reveals such degree combinations as marketing with: languages, business studies, fashion, economics, law, psychology, public relations, tourism, hospitality, leisure or retail, events and arts, e-business technology, ICT, food and drink, media, journalism, communication, bio-sciences, computing, early childhood studies, English, environmental science, music, graphic design, human resource management, product design & innovation, advertising, web-based systems. There's something for everyone!

But even with a degree, you'll have to get some experience, and if you want to move upwards in the marketing world you will need to get some professional qualifications from the appropriate body.

Professional organisations
CIM

The Chartered Institute of Marketing is widely recognised as being the foremost national marketing organisation in the UK. The CIM is well respected in South East Asia, Australia and elsewhere overseas where CIM qualifications – as in the UK – are used as professional standards or benchmarks for everybody in the industry from newcomers to experienced marketers.

The 'qualification ladder' starts with the Introductory Certificate in Marketing which is open to anyone considering their first steps in what might become a marketing career. Experience is not essential and both the teaching and subject matter are geared to suit someone who has a minimal amount of knowledge about the process of marketing. In essence, this is a qualification that provides you with the essentials of marketing theory, and gives you some practical knowledge to get you started in the workplace.

As you can see from the following table the age groups and skill levels for students taking the various CIM qualifications will be roughly equivalent to the ages and abilities of those students taking GCSEs, A levels (Introductory Certificate), Higher Education (HE) diplomas and the first year of a degree (Professional Certificate), university degrees (Professional Diploma) and academically and professionally experienced people taking Master's degrees and Doctorates (Chartered Postgraduate Diploma in Marketing).

■ The Professional Certificate in Marketing is for those who have secured their first job and would like to get promotion. It gives the student an in-depth knowledge of understanding customers, how to conduct research, manage a marketing budget and write a marketing plan.

■ The third level, the Professional Diploma in Marketing is for the marketer with aspirations for management. The subject matter begins to get more complex at this point which is why the equivalent qualification noted in the table overleaf is at university degree level. The students that take the Professional Diploma will learn how to implement strategy, measure and evaluate success and fully understand the different functions of marketing within the commercial sector and how the marketing process impacts upon various business models.

■ There are specialist courses such as the e-Marketing Award which provides the specialist marketer with a grounding in IT related marketing activities dealing with issues such as research, e-based sales, marketing plans and all aspects of web related marketing.

■ The Diploma in Tourism Marketing provides the student with a good range of relevant marketing and business skills for those entering the leisure industry and experienced individuals who wish to set the pace and actually create strategy at the highest levels have the Chartered Postgraduate Diploma and Chartered Marketer status to aim for.

See Resources section for contact details for the CIM.

Other professional bodies

You may consider other organisations, depending on the area you specialise in. Their requirements for membership and accreditation vary, so you should research them when you are drawing up your action plan.

Age groups and skill levels for students taking CIM qualifications

qualification (equivalent level)	age (will vary)	ideal for...	what is it?
Introductory Certificate in Marketing (A level)	17–20+	Those people who are just starting out in their marketing careers, secretarial or administrative roles, people on the edge of marketing, event and other activities such as sales. PAs and other individuals working alongside the marketing department.	The Introductory Certificate in Marketing is for all those who want to find out more about marketing – whether you're in a job that involves the discipline or not. You will know what marketing consists of and be able to develop your knowledge and skills to benefit your employer (or your business).
Professional Certificate in Marketing (HE diplomas, university first year of a degree, level 4/5 BTEC)	19–23+	This qualification is for those working in support of marketing professionals, such as marketing assistance, where you are involved to a lesser extent in day-to-day marketing activities.	You will gain hands-on practical skills and knowledge which will enable you to become involved in day-to-day marketing activities.

Professional Diploma in Marketing (University degrees, level 6/7 BTEC)	19–23+	Marketers with aspirations to formulate and implement marketing strategy and those who are seeking managerial responsibility for top accounts departments, and agencies (eg marketing executives and business development managers).	Passing these exams and obtaining this much sought-after qualification will bring you much closer to management level. This qualification places a considerable emphasis on effective management and business skills and it is regarded as the benchmark for companies who seek ambitious and capable marketing professionals.
Chartered Postgraduate Diploma in Marketing (Postgraduate diplomas and certificates, Masters)	23+	This diploma is for those individuals who seek strategic management roles and who aspire to the top level of achievement with this organisation and in the marketing profession.	This is a very difficult marketing qualification to obtain and those that achieve this level can use the Chartered Marketer status label which is a widely recognised professional achievement.

The **Incorporated Society of British Advertisers (ISBA)** offers training designed to bridge the gap between what people learn in their academic studies, and the skills they need to do their job in the world of advertising. They run training workshops at introductory and advanced levels in a range of subjects and skills.

The **Institute of Practitioners in Advertising (IPA)** offers a full training and professional development programme of specially designed training courses and workshops for core business skills and the latest theory and practice for people working in its member agencies.

The **Internet Advertising Bureau (IAB)** is the trade association for the internet marketing industry and works in collaboration with a number of reputable digital training companies to provide a wide selection of internet marketing courses, as well as workshops and seminars.

The **Institute of Sales Promotion (ISP)** represents the UK marketing industry with a mission to protect, promote and progress effective sales promotion across all media channels. It offers training and qualifications in promotional and interactive marketing, motivation, experiential marketing and digital promotions.

The **Market Research Society (MRS)** has members in more than 70 countries, and is for those providing or using market, social and opinion research, and business intelligence, market analysis, customer insight and consultancy.

MRS is recognised by the UK government as an awarding body for vocationally-related qualifications in market and social research, designed to suit candidates just starting out with an interest in market research or those with experience looking for further professional development.

The **Institute of Direct Marketing (IDM)** is an educational organisation for the professional development of direct, data and digital marketing. It offers professional membership, qualifications and training in such topics as: digital marketing, direct and interactive marketing, integrated marketing communications, B2B marketing (business to business), and applied marketing analytics.

The **Direct Marketing Association (DMA)** has developed a number of industry accreditation schemes as part of the ongoing drive to improve standards within the industry.

The role of the **Direct Selling Association (DSA)** is to promote direct selling and uphold the highest standards of good practice by its member companies through its codes of practice.

GETTING YOUR FIRST JOB IN MARKETING

Work experience

Getting experience in your chosen area of work has at least two benefits. It lets you find out if you have made the right decision about the kind of work you will be happy doing, and it also supports you finding a permanent position. You may try to get a short placement before you take any relevant qualifications or when newly qualified.

> 'The only job where you start at the top is digging a hole.'
>
> Anon

CIM has a career partner scheme aimed at students who wish to get into marketing. It is free and designed to help you get started in the profession. There's general advice about working in the industry, and how to get your foot in the door by making your CV and job application really stand out. Since experience counts for a lot, you can also take advantage of their marketing placement service too. All the details can be found on the CIM website: www.cim.co.uk/cpd/getintomrkt.aspx

You can also directly contact large and medium-size organisations (those likely to have marketing departments of a reasonable size) in your local area to see if they would be willing to take someone on in a work experience placement. It might also be worth contacting your local CIM branch to ask if they know of any work experience opportunities in their area.

An internet search also yields a variety of possibilities. For example, there is a scheme called STRIDE run by Bournemouth University. It arranges short placements of one to six months for graduates to undertake work that the employer may not normally have the time or resources to complete.

When you undertake work experience you could be involved in a very specific project, which could increase your special skills, or you may just get a feel for the general tasks, but you will gain valuable experience for your CV and you never know, the employer may take you on as a permanent recruit!

The cream of the crop

Some agencies run their own specialist training programmes. There can be huge competition to get a place on these schemes: for example Ogilvy & Mather only takes up to ten new trainees each year. But of course the experience they offer is second to none and can be the launch pad for a very successful career. Gary Leih describes more about this in his interview in Chapter Six.

Paid work

Whether you have some specific marketing qualifications or not, you are going to want a job. You could try approaching large companies speculatively see if they will consider you for their in-house department. Or try marketing or advertising or research agencies, and other specialist areas if that is what interests you. For this you will need a carefully crafted CV and letter; advice on this is readily available in other places, such as through school, college and university careers' centres and on professional organisation websites. CIM offer a career partner scheme, which includes help with CV preparation.

However, the norm towards the end of your university education, or when you want to get the first job in your marketing career, is to check through the papers every day for adverts which are placed by both company HR departments and recruitment agencies. You can search on the internet for specialist marketing recruitment agencies where you can register your CV, such as the sales and marketing network and the professional marketing network www.professionalnetworkmarketing.com.

CAREER PROGRESSION

It seems to me that as you get experience in the marketing world you are more likely to be contacted by the very sophisticated head-hunting agencies that exist across the commercial sector these days. This is especially true of marketing; everybody I have spoken to at the peak of their careers have used head-hunting agencies to transfer allegiances (see interviews in the next chapter). And things are moving on from here as well because sophisticated networking websites now exist, where members update their working histories, achievements and CVs for all to see, and this is probably the first place a CEO would look for his next top recruit to a marketing, advertising or sales team.

It is also important to bear in mind the crucial nature of the 'mentor' in marketing, and especially in sales. This is where a rising star takes his own team with him every time he makes a move, or calls old buddies to make up a team. It's quite common for a whole group of people to leave at the same time, and this often happens because one individual is taking the pick of the team with him or her when they go. They will often make it a condition of their new employment, because the people they take with them are tried and trusted. The mentor knows that the team will deliver the results that benefit them all.

Is also important to remember that word-of-mouth plays a huge part as people get higher up the 'food chain'. As you gain experience and make a network of contacts across both the marketing and specific industry sectors, you may find that you reputation goes before you, and you may even be head-hunted. If you are recruiting and know someone's a flyer, you know their quality, then you can be confident that they will perform, get results, and make you look good if you introduce them into your own company. You will also know that a class act can hit the ground running, and this is all-important in results driven environments like sales.

Because of this, some managers poach other people's teams. There's rarely any truce, and no apologies are forthcoming. I remember sales teams being decimated because of a mass exodus to a company offering more money for the same work.

Rungs on the ladder

People in marketing generally change jobs more frequently and this varies again within marketing, advertising and sales. You are likely to change jobs on average every four years or less and in sales it is probably more like three years or under because of the transient nature of the sales arena. If you don't move every three years in sales something is probably wrong and you're about to go stale or you will shortly become yesterday's news and the target of a new manager's broom.

While there is no such thing as a typical marketing career, there can be a basic pattern to it. No matter what your educational achievements, you are likely to start as a marketing assistant of some kind – as part of an in-house department, or in an agency (which may specialise in certain aspects such as advertising, or e-marketing). Here you'll cut your teeth on all sorts of tasks, mundane and interesting, while you learn about what goes on and your employer learns about you and what you are capable of. Nothing beats this kind of experience as a preparation and basis of a good career. After a period of time you will move up a step and be responsible for a particular area of work or projects.

Depending on the size of organisation you are in or move to, the next step may be to a junior management post, or to head of a department. From here, if you are in-house, the next step would actually be away from marketing and into general management. Often, people who reach this level in an agency move out and set up their own business. As we see in our interviews, that entrepreneurial spirit may emerge earlier too. And of course there are many marketers who will remain employed and happy in the middle ranks.

The route to success, whether it's working your way up a company or agency structure, or starting out on your own, relies on your continually growing knowledge, your enthusiasm, and of course a lot of hard work. These qualities will be recognised by management, head-hunters and recruitment panels alike.

All ambitious executives need to create and constantly adapt a proactive strategy for upward mobility or progression up the promotional ladder. A passive approach of simply waiting for someone to come along and offer a job isn't going to be very effective.

For example, people can improve their chances of being head-hunted by cultivating contacts within a trusted and known agency and keeping this channel of communication open. Networking events are run by various organisations to facilitate communication and create referral business. So join the best one. Conferences and colleagues will also provide the keen marketer with new opportunities.

Sometimes the old tried and trusted concept of patronage still works well, although if the star of your mentor wanes you may have a problem!

You may be able to swap roles (eg from research to advertising) as you go up the ladder, thus gaining additional experience and contacts, not to mention avoiding or sidestepping potential 'bottlenecks' in the promotional journey.

Don't forget the possibilities of setting up on your own and starting your own business (see *Working for Yourself Uncovered* in the same series). This happens all the time when opportunities are created by circumstance not exploited by the parent company (and with management buyout, for example) leaving the door open for a far sighted employee who had a hankering for their own business.

Of course there are all sorts of other ways to help yourself move up that promotional ladder; these ideas are to serve as a starting point only.

Chapter Six
REAL MARKETERS

I remember a marketing student who was diligently ploughing her way through the course reading list she had been given saying, 'So far, so much theory,' by which she meant that the reading list contained what appeared to be a lot of theory and in her words 'not enough about real people'.

This of course may have been a fault of that particular reading list, and the person who put it together, namely me. So I decided to try and rectify the situation by getting on the phone to invite some real marketers into class to help with a couple of lectures a week. The reaction of the students was very positive. They thoroughly enjoyed hearing about the experiences of people first hand – many of whom are doing extremely well in the business and are very knowledgeable. The value of learning about the experiences of people who are active in the business to which you aspire led me to include the following case studies in the book.

CASE STUDIES

Of course, the process of getting real people involved in this book wasn't as easy as it first appeared. For a start, they are busy people; Gary Leih for instance, is the Chairman and CEO of Ogilvy UK, and runs a group of specialist companies involved in practically every communications discipline there is, from advertising, direct marketing, PR and sales promotion to design, interactive, studio and creative work, the list goes on… I was lucky that he had the time to talk to me and I was particularly pleased that he found the time, not only because the advice he has to give to those who want to work in marketing is obviously extremely relevant, but also because in this atmosphere of economic doom and gloom it was great to hear from someone like Gary who seems to love what he does and still seems to relish the everyday challenges of a career in marketing.

Who to ask

It was quite tricky deciding who it would be best to interview, and after further discussions I came to the conclusion that it would be best to make sure that we have some first hand experiences of some key areas in the book, namely: research, advertising, direct sales and customer service and some more specific roles such as an event management. These choices clearly do not cover the whole spectrum of career options, so if you are interested in a marketing discipline not covered by one of the interviews have a look at the Resources section, where I have listed organisations that can help and advise you.

Not everybody in marketing works for a big company and is therefore an employee. There are a lot of self-employed people out there who run their own small to medium-size marketing businesses. It would be wrong to exclude them because they are important and have different things to say to the would-be marketer, so I decided to make sure that I included a couple of interviews with people who run their own business.

Leanne Bramhall, Director of Lime Juice Marketing, a small agency

Company profile

Lime Juice Marketing was established in 2006 when award winning marketeer Leane Bramhall and Kerry Sterne, the brains behind Sphere Marketing and Kerry Sterne In House Sales, joined forces to bring a new marketing company to the South West, with the aim of stimulating the growth of local businesses to create a positive effect on the local economy. The young, creative and energetic team offers marketing, public relations, copy writing, branding, on-line marketing, creative design and event management.

Career profile

Business graduate Leane began her career working on a project basis for various companies including Bournemouth University. She continued to gain experience of marketing and business management across a range of sectors from a large multi-national to SMEs.

Having moved from Dorset in 2004, Leane now works with clients across Devon and Cornwall at strategic planning level as well as managing marketing implementation and evaluation. Her latest success was being awarded Network of Women, Young Entrepreneur of the Year. She is an active member of the Chartered Institute of Marketing and has recently been nominated as Vice Chair for Cornwall CIM.

AR   Thank you for coming today can you tell us what you are doing now?

LB   I am now working in a company called Lime Juice Marketing that is about six months old; I am working in a self-employed capacity and it is a marketing and sales agency that aims to work alongside local businesses. When I say local, I am talking about Devon and stretching into Cornwall to work alongside them as an outsourced sales and marketing department.

AR   What sort of things do you do for these businesses?

LB   Work alongside the directors of the company in their strategy and planning stages and then from planning through to implementation – so full service in that sense.

AR   A sort of 'marketing MOT'?

LB   Yes, help identify any areas that they are weaker on, so they can use our expertise.

AR   What was your first job?

LB   My first job was waitressing at £2.50 per hour – I worked so hard for that money! (laughs)

AR   So what attracted you to marketing in the first place?

LB   I had a natural interest in business and soon realised how important marketing was to each of the businesses that I was working in. It went on from there, really. I had read how marketing fits into business management and liked what I read.

AR   **Did you go to university?**

LB   Yes, Exeter University, studying biology.

AR   **So not marketing?**

LB   No! I found business came naturally to me and I enjoy it.

AR   **Tell us about your first marketing role and how you got it.**

LB   It was at Bournemouth University, and I got it after quite a gruelling interview with the Head of the Department at the time. They were looking for a six month maternity cover placement, classed as a PR and marketing consultancy role.

AR   **General dogsbody?**

LB   It did start out that way, but they also gave me some really good projects that I could get my teeth into, and at that point it really just consolidated my thoughts about marketing and that was it! I was absolutely hungry for it, and I loved the role.

AR   **It sounds like you had a job epiphany; what moment was it, or what job did he give you that convinced you?**

LB   It was mixture of two things at the time actually. It was the fact that I started to work really well with them and they gave me a project to launch a new service they had for second year students. They gave it to me as a full project to run with, in whatever way I wanted. It was to launch a 'student business scheme' to allow second year students to experience setting up a business or work in a local business. The pay was minimal but it was a really good way for them to gain the practical skills they need in business.

The key objective was to get as many students involved as possible. I was really passionate about it as I felt it was a great idea. I had freedom to manage myself and run things the way that I wanted so I set up regular marketing meetings to provide project updates and gain senior management input.

AR   **How long had you worked for them when this happened?**

LB   On that project it was about three months, but I was with them for about six months in total.

AR   **So that was a good opportunity to prove yourself?**

LB   Yes, it went very well and I got some glowing references.

AR   **Was there another project that you enjoyed?**

LB   Yes, it was working on their in-house magazine; they needed some topical stories to go in there.

AR   **Had you ever done that before?**

LB   No (laughs).

AR   **That's fascinating and next?**

LB   After that I went travelling, then when I came back I temped while applying for career progression roles. I worked in advertising sales for a little while: doing the donkey work, getting on the phones, telesales, going out meeting clients – hard sales.

AR   **What was this for?**

LB   It was for a magazine that was aimed at the youth entertainment market; pubs, clubs, nights out, that sort of thing.

AR   **You picked a tough one to come back to!**

LB   Yes – I really didn't enjoy that job if I am honest.

AR   **But good experience and learning good lessons?**

LB   Yes, absolutely. Actually if I am now booking advertising on behalf of a client I know they are more than ready to negotiate on costs. But it was really tough sales and I am not actually a tough sales character, so it didn't come naturally to me.

AR   **So how long did you have that job?**

LB   Two and a half months – not very long at all.

AR   **But still a good learning process?**

LB   Yes – I learnt all about the media, so to speak, which really helped me out. From there I was offered the interview with a large multi-national company.

AR   **And did you see that job advertised in the paper?**

LB   No, I was sort of head-hunted actually. I put my CV on a random website and hadn't really thought that much about it. Then I got a phone call from a lady saying that she had a great job, to which I said 'yeah, yeah, I am sure you do!...' I went for two interviews – the first was in Taunton and I was half an hour late for it! Luckily they knew that there was an accident down the motorway.

AR   **That's horrible isn't it?**

LB   Oh, I turned up flustered and bright red because I hate being late – it does look so unprofessional. But it went really well with the two people interviewing me. The second interview was more hands on – they were testing me as to whether I was listening to them.

AR   **Were there role plays and so on?**

LB   Yes, and a personality test.

AR   **So this was your third marketing role. How did it go from day one? What were you doing?**

LB   Before I was allowed into the marketing department I spent nine months out on the road, which I loved.

AR   **Who with? Doing what?**

LB   Just me doing sales – well what they class as sales; it's actually account management: going into the shops, making sure they have got all the new and latest stands, the equipment they need, the latest product updates... I just loved it. I was my own manager and I basically got to go round talking to people. And that's all it was – finding out what they needed and delivering it.

AR   **Were you good at it?**

LB   Yes – I didn't do too badly actually. I was quite surprised!

AR   **Tell me more about this company. What happened after the road trip?**

LB   After the road trip I was interviewed again (laughs) and then promoted to the marketing department in my first formal marketing role, which was as marketing assistant on a dental brand. I learnt so many things there, really trained from the bottom up, and after just over 12 months I was promoted again. Then after two years I was promoted again, and at that point I thought, 'if I don't leave now and do my own thing I am not sure that I ever will'.

AR   **So let's consider all three roles that you have had so far: what have you liked – and just as importantly, what have you disliked about the marketing roles that you have had?**

LB   Liked: there are so many things I like about marketing but the overriding thing is the challenge and flexibility of every single day. It's not the same; you don't get up in the morning at 8am and have your tea break at 11am. It's not like that. You can't plan your day like that. There are so many different things and you get to meet so many different people. Its never boring, its always changing. In marketing you have to constantly learn…

AR   **Can you give us an example of how a day varied?**

LB   One minute I would be in Plymouth, presenting to the sales team and then in the afternoon preparing for the next product launch. Then the next day I could be in London presenting to the advertising agency. So in that sense it is so very different. One day I would be up at 5am to get the train to London and the next day I would be up at 7am to be in the office. It is just so different all the time. Often my days involve really detailed work, but I also work on the whiz-bang projects, for example launching a product or managing a sponsorship deal.

AR   **These are the sorts of things you were doing on a daily basis?**

LB   Yes. The more detailed work involved in day-to-day brand management, like having to watch a product performance on a daily basis. We were expected to know exactly where you are and where you planned to. Often the managing director would stop you in a corridor and ask 'how's that product going?' or 'what's the latest sales push?' So you are just expected to know right up to the latest second.

AR   **So variety is something you like, but is there something you don't like so much about some of the roles you have had?**

LB   Data analysis! It is hard work, it is time consuming, it's detailed. It's just a bit of a headache and although it is essential, it's not one of the things I relish.

AR   **You mean where you have done some research, questionnaires for example, and you have to interpret the results, is that right?**

LB   Yes, absolutely.

AR   What part of your marketing roles have motivated you?

LB   Being able to manage myself. Being trusted to do the job.

AR   That's come up before – people like to be asked to do
      something and then be given the space in which to do it.

LB   Yes. I don't like to be managed too closely. When I was much
      younger (back to waitressing) I was managed so closely it made
      me feel quite dumb and patronised and I didn't deal with that
      particularly well. Ever since then it has been ingrained. If I am left
      to manage the job, and understand what the timelines are and
      the deliverables, and you let me get on with it so I can feed back
      at regular intervals, I get more efficient. I think that is why I like
      working for myself.

AR   Yes I can see in marketing you stand or fall by the latest
      project. This is OK?

LB   Yes.

AR   So if someone said to you 'what does it take to be
      successful in marketing' what would you say?

LB   Be driven. Marketing changes so often and you need to keep
      learning and keep staying on top of things and keep going,
      you have to be driven and motivated. Whether you are self-
      employed or in a big organisation you have to be driven.

AR   When you were helping recruit, what do you think your
      bosses, were looking for?

LB   A mixture of things: personable people, good people
      management skills as well – as a marketer you are often
      managing teams of people, working with sales teams. Also
      key is an eye for detail and obviously, above all, being a good
      communicator, whether written or verbal.

AR   Let's say at the multi-national you work for, what was the
      recruitment process? How did people join? Did they get
      these jobs through the papers or were they through an
      agency?

LB   Quite often this was managed through agencies as they found it
      easier to trawl through CVs if there were just five or so from an
      agency rather than the 500 they would get if using the paper.

AR   **And what about the university? Did they use agencies?**

LB   A mixture, both through the local paper and through agencies.

AR   **What sort of roles are there for those entering marketing?**

LB   At the bottom as marketing assistants, dealing with marketing admin, the leg work, the hard work stuff!

AR   **If I was looking for advice and I said I was considering a career in marketing, what advice would you give me?**

LB   I would probably first find out what it is you want out of a career, so that I understood whether a career in marketing was actually the right approach for you. But if that was done and marketing was definitely the right career for you, I would say, 'get as much experience as possible across as many businesses as possible to begin with before you settle down into the career progression through a national company'.

AR   **So, you have started a business?**

LB   Yes, I was in a fantastic business to work for; however, I had aspirations beyond that role. At the time I noticed so many other local businesses that I felt I could help. It got to the point that, having always wanted to run my own company it was time to do it: I am glad I have done it now.

AR   **You set the company up when?**

LB   Two years ago I went self-employed and set up a company called Sphere Marketing and six months ago I joined forces with someone to form Lime Juice Marketing.

AR   **And what are you doing now?**

LB   I am working with several smaller local businesses as an outsourced marketing department. I go in there as marketing manager, setting up long term marketing plans.

AR   **So they can use you when they need you, then drop you, then link up again when it suits them?**

LB   Yes. It is nice to have clients on a retainer, but as an external marketing manager they don't have to retain me. It depends on what the client needs.

AR **Can you give us an example of something you have really enjoyed lately?**

LB   The latest one I have done is on a disaster recovery suite, which is aimed at local businesses. I had to do a lot of market research to understand the best way to approach the market, prior to presenting to the Board. We went through the whole planning process from scratch, which I really enjoyed. I had the market research and data analysis completed up front and this provided me with the insights and direction for the marketing planning. The market is really interesting and exciting things have come out of it. We are now just entering the project management and implementation phase to make it happen. They are a business continuity management company. It works with companies so that if disaster should strike they have another office that they could come to. This saves down time and lost business.

AR **So you are helping to put this together? You are enjoying it?**

LB   Yes – I love it!

AR **What is it about this project that you like?**

LB   Working with self-employed people is great. I wasn't getting that in my previous roles. A different kind of person runs their own business…

AR **Finally, what is the best bit in marketing so far? Best moment, achievement so far?**

LB   Best moment was launching a sponsorship with the Ducatti team bikes and presenting in front of a couple of hundred people at a large hotel near Cardiff; it was quite amazing. Also winning an award at the end of one of the annual company gatherings, for Leadership Innovation. Finally, the latest award I won was from the Network of Women, Young Entrepreneur of the Year, which was fantastic as people didn't have to vote for me.

AR **Worst moment?**

LB   Do you know what, after setting up for myself I won a contract for four months then went two months without any work, and that scared me!

Contact details

Leanne Bramhall
Lime Juice Marketing
Airport Business Centre
10 Thornbury Road
Estover
Plymouth PL6 7PP
Tel: 05601 255 581
info@limejuicemarketing.co.uk
www.limejuicemarketing.co.uk

....

Clive Hammett, Director, iMedia Marketing Limited

Company profile

iMedia Marketing Limited is a web development company offering
services that range from website design to pay-per-click marketing,
to custom software development.

iMedia use a pool of developers based in the South West who work on a
wide range of applications, databases, and technologies.

Career profile

Clive Hammett has developed his career [see questions 1–4 below] from
rocket scientist and physicist through a very successful sales series to his
current position as director of a web-based marketing company doing
the following jobs for his clients.

■   Different types of websites, delivery options and costs.

■   Improving websites and search engine optimisation.

■   Driving traffic to the site.

■   Email campaigns and managing mailing lists effectively.

■   Paid advertising options and costs/benefits.

■   Measuring effectiveness.

AR   **Can I ask you a bit about how you got started and what
was your first job?**

CH   My first job was a rocket scientist! I got a degree in physics with a view to joining the air force, but went into missile design for the Ministry of Defence instead.

       I then worked for Plessey in defence and did sales and marketing for them. I was the marketing manager for Plessey for four or five years.

AR   **Where did you go from there?**

CH   I joined a small company who distributed and tested software systems. They built and sold complex IT systems.

AR   **What attracted you to this job?**

CH   I realised I could double my salary (laughs) and have a company car! Also it was very challenging as it was a small company and I could make my mark – I had to get the business – there was nowhere to hide like there may be in larger companies.

AR   **What drew you to sales?**

CH   I love meeting people and working out how I can help them. I get a real buzz when I think I can offer something people really want.

AR   **Was it difficult to make the transition from the technical, scientific side to the sales?**

CH   I had to learn the necessary administration skills, to enable me to write proposals etc. The transfer from 'tech head' to sales needed a little adjustment.

AR   **What did you do next?**

CH   Well, from that company, where I cut my teeth in sales, I moved on to other companies, gaining experience and getting better at what I did. I went to Instrumatic, and built up a team of 43 sales staff from a small beginning. We had a great marketing department which made the good sales possible.

AR   **What qualifications do you need to go into sales?**

CH   You need to have a sound background in the field you are selling for. It's crucial you understand your product, whether it's insurance or computers.

AR   **How would be the best way to gain entry into sales?**

CH   It's difficult because you need experience. I was involved in recruiting and I wouldn't even look at someone without experience. It's essential that you have the knowledge and understanding of what you are selling, and if they are there then I would be looking for personality, hunger, drive, enthusiasm and the ability to get on with people.

AR   How would you decide whether someone had all these personal qualities?

CH   You may ask about previous experience and see how they respond. You could ask how much money they need to live off, to find out how hungry they would be to top up their basic salary, by gaining sales – how big is your mortgage etc. No sales person should be happy living off their basic wage!

AR   Can you explain how sales people need to be different from other marketers?

CH   I think in marketing you need to be more literate and personable, but obviously you still need lots of drive and enthusiasm. There are very different skills involved. Sales take the leads set by marketing and make it happen! Sales are more ruthless than marketing.

AR   What advice would you give to someone who is starting out in sales?

CH   I would say it's best to look for a new, small, interesting company who are also just starting out. Look for a mentor who is a visionary and learn from them. If the new company is looking to push a new project, it's likely to be exciting and a strong learning environment. You can gain lots of experience within the company and aim to stay a couple of years. Sales tend to be quite transient, so people do move on quite quickly. You need to think about your goals and what you want from a job. If you work for larger companies, you tend to get pigeon holed. You need to look for opportunities and make things happen!

AR   What advice would you give to anyone in sales or marketing?

CH   Well, a company's fortunes always change. There is re-organisation, you may get fired, and you may get bored. Don't stay too long in one company. Just learn as much as you can, work out how to maximise how much you earn. You will find that

after a couple of years your performance and drive will decline
– it's inevitable. Even if you do a good job, things change, so try
to move when you are doing well. This isn't always possible, as
you quite often don't have the time or energy to apply for jobs.
Sales is stressful and hard work if you want to do well.

AR **Any other thoughts you would pass on to anyone thinking
of going into sales?**

CH It's often the case in marketing that finding yourself a mentor
is a tremendous help. Someone to look up to and learn from,
someone who can help you rise through the ranks by taking you
with them as part of their team.

AR **So, tell me what does a web-based marketing company
like iMedia Marketing offer?**

CH We help small and medium sized businesses get business
through the web. Yes, we build websites – they are great
looking and work well, but our focus, which is generally
overlooked by clients and web-developers alike, is to make
sure they are effective in attracting visitors in the first place.
Great graphics are no good if no-one sees them. So we
provide search engine optimised (SEO) websites. And we offer
pay-per-click PPC and email marketing services too.

We have people with experience of running high street shops,
so we can advise about effective approaches to do with the
whole business. But what matters is getting quality visitors to
the website, and then having a website with a clear message
and easy navigation which converts visitors into clients.

AR **How is the marketing of companies and products
changing?**

CH Within our niche, small and medium sized companies, we are
seeing a decline in high street sales, and growth between 24%
and 25% in internet based sales. So businesses need to have
an internet presence.

Many businesses have websites, but frankly from the analysis
we have done on many of them, they are dated, ineffective,
and not designed to attract business. We are seeing a growth
in redevelopment, with improvement of SEO and added PPC
services on existing sites.

Many companies assumed that having a website was good
enough and were happy to self-build, or use a friend or family

member to knock up their website for them. We have analysed such websites and demonstrated that 93% of the developers have no awareness of correct SEO techniques.

AR   **Why is this important?**

CH   Well, good SEO is vital if you hope that someone who does not know your web address and searches on the web will find you. The web is highly competitive, typically there may be 100,000 relevant web pages for the keywords for a specific business, but if your website does not appear in, say, the top eight listings then it is wasted. Many professionally built websites are no better.

AR   **And pay-per-click?**

CH   Pay-per-click is not cost-effective for very low volume businesses, but if it's done well it's a great, and often the best way, to spend a marketing budget.

Done properly you will know that for every £100 spent you gain say £1,000 in sales – that beats the old joke that 50% of a marketing budget is wasted, the problem is you do not know what 50%!

AR   **What about email marketing, and other new approaches?**

CH   Very few companies yet use email marketing regularly (less than 15%) to keep existing customers informed and get further sales, but interest is increasing.

We are seeing a massive uptake in the use of video on websites – say for customer references and on social networking websites like Youtube. These, along with blogs and twitter, are creating networks of people which can be easy to market to and influence. Anyone now can set themselves up as an expert and get an audience. The key is not to sell but to get people to visit your website which does the selling.

AR   **What is driving these developments?**

CH   People are having good ideas for businesses; often they have redundancy money, and realise that they can go to market via the web. Highly powerful ecommerce websites are now available for only a few thousand pounds, and they are easy for non-technical people to manage. So more and more people are going to market. Maybe the UK will change from being a 'nation of shopkeepers' to a 'nation of webmasters'.

AR	What does the future hold in the cyber marketing world?
CH	Sorry I don't know. There is bound to be some new service or technology that comes out of the blue. Things are constantly evolving.
AR	**If someone wanted to get into internet marketing as a career choice, what advice would you give them?**
CH	Obviously become knowledgeable about the topic, get trained up, get experience, find a company willing to take you on. A lot of people out there in internet marketing have been self-taught.
AR	**Can you describe a favourite moment in your career?**
CH	That is very difficult – I don't think I can. I'm never satisfied – as soon as one project is finished I'm ready to move on to the next!
AR	**So, looking back on your career are you happy with what you see?**
CH	Yes, it is a great career. I've always got a buzz from helping people. I think marketing has a unique set of challenges.

Contact details

Clive Hammett, Director
Tel: 01803 205649
www.imediamarketing.co.uk
clive.hammett@imediamarketing.co.uk

....

Robert Rush, Managing Director, PFA Research

Company profile

PFA Research provides organisations with essential market intelligence to allow them to evaluate, quantify and address their market and customers. They use proven market research and consultancy practice: face-to-face market research, focus groups, mystery shopping, quantitative telephone surveys. These primary research techniques are underpinned with secondary research and literature reviews as necessary. PFA specialises in business-to-business and public opinion polling.

Personal/career profile

Robert Rush is an experienced Project Manager and Research Consultant and has been a member of PFA Research since 1992. He went to university in Huddersfield and has settled in the other end of the country, namely Cornwall. He is now the Managing Director of PFA Research and specialises in evidence-led approaches to business and market planning strategy development.

AR   **Thanks for coming along, we'd better start straight away with the business. Please tell me about it.**

RR   Well, PFA is what the industry would term a 'full service market research engine' business; it's all about helping other businesses, taking evidence that relates to their marketing and business planning, rather than relying on a gut feeling.

AR   **Look before you leap?**

RR   Before you leap, exactly. It's good to have your gut feel, which gives you your drive, but at some point you've got to take a reality check; look at the numbers, look at the evidence and make sure that you are actually steering in the right direction.

AR   **Otherwise you're wasting money?**

RR   Yes. We cover a whole range of things. Most of our work is surveys, telephone based; lots of it is business-to-business or it's postal, huge volumes of paper questionnaires coming back through the post.

AR   **External mail?**

RR   Yes, but we also do online surveys. Usually it's about understanding and seeing what the objectives of the problem are, and understanding the best ways to collect that data.

AR   **How long have you been in business?**

RR   This is the 18th year for the company.

AR   **18 years?**

RR   Yes, I joined on it's very first day in 1992, the first proper day it was set up.

AR   **And you own it?**

RR   I partly own it.

AR   **How is it managed?**

RR   All internally managed. I was just looking at an email in response to a tender and they wanted to put clarification as to how many people are in the company; we have a nucleus of about three and then the chairman. Then we have a whole bank of people, some of them have been with us for years. We don't sub out much, it's all managed and run internally and they are our employees.

AR   **And you cover the whole of the South West?**

RR   Yes, and nationally we currently have clients in Cheshire, Manchester, the South East and Reading.

AR   **As you well know, this book is for people that are coming into the business and they're considering what to do. It might help them if they understood what attracted you to marketing and how you ended up in it in the first place.**

RR   Yes. I'm a graduate in electronics and information engineering, that's what I studied. I was always going to be a software engineer. Well that's what I thought I was going to do, but I graduated in 1991 during the last recession – not a really good start, and it got tough. PFA, a management consultancy from London, were setting up a research business in Bodmin, and they were interested in finding telephone researchers who could use a telephone and had some understanding of telecoms, computers and conference speaking with senior people. Not that I'd ever really done that, but I thought, 'Ok I'll give it a go, I'll do that for a couple of years then go and get a proper job.'

AR   **So many marketing people have said that...**

RR   Yes, that's right. I'm not sure whether I was one of their first choices, as they recruited a whole team, but I think because I could find my way around a computer, in those days, it did help. I found I could always deal with it; I have a logical mind, an analytical mind. I could do it and make things work, so I was useful to have around. I added software and crunched the data and moved what was coming out of the interviews, so they could use it. They thought it might be useful to have me around as a bit of a technician and I think as time went on that was it.

AR   **You found your niche?**

RR   Yes; although I didn't know that I was finding my niche, that I was going to end up in a business I would grow to love.

The company was specialised in the early days, focussed on technology sectors, and as I was from a technical background it was a nice fit. I certainly didn't see myself as a marketer or realise at that time that I was going to end up as one!

AR   And that's when you got your first proper job in marketing and promotion too I suppose?

RR   Well I think in small businesses it tends to be a little bit more organic, you need to get down and scrub the deck.

AR   What do you like and dislike about the current role?

RR   I think the likes and dislikes are the same, the challenge. I've come a long way and the roles are very different. Now it's about going out and getting the business, it's about the chase, it's about success. You have to keep re-evaluating your role. I think I came to a decision about six months ago that I have possibly come a little too far away from the coal face. It was all very well going in at the beginning, analysing your needs in market research then going back, handing it over to somebody to write it all up, then going back and saying here are your results, but you haven't really been involved in it that much. So I took a re-evaluation.

AR   You're a bit more involved in the day-to-day running?

RR   I try to be. It's a very small company anyway, so you're always really involved but it's about getting back into the thick of it. I really love doing the networking, the actual going out and meeting people. If anyone phones up and says it would be really interesting to get together for a chat, I would go because for me that's the really interesting part of the job.

AR   The networking you enjoy – it's a good part of the business?

RR   Yes, it's almost my social life. If you have one or two events in the evening, going out, I really enjoy it.

AR   And motivation – you're very people orientated, is there anything else that motivates you?

RR   The reality of the motivation is more than about a small business; I suppose it is 'how is the mortgage going to get paid if you don't'. There is no bigger motivation than that!

AR   That's important to us all.

RR   When you work backwards from that, it's all that you have to do. I just really love my job. It's always changing. Finding out what others think…

AR **People, business, marketing – if you do it right, it generally pays the way.**

RR It's an interesting thing and you really should understand motivation. I don't understand the work/life thing; when you enjoy what you do, to me it's all the same. If you're happy in one, if you've got the work right, it's all part of fulfilling life. You have to get the balance and understand the things you're thankful for. I'm grateful for the family, I'm grateful for the fact that when we finish today I can go back to the team in the office who are keeping things going.

AR **If someone was sitting here and you were advising, and they asked you what it took to be successful in marketing, I presume some of the answers would be what you've already given me, but is there anything else you could add?**

RR Yes, sometimes you just have to do it. I'm trying to think who coined the phrase 'ready, aim, fire'. You know sometimes you just have to go for it, you can spend so much time going aim, aim, aim, trying to get things right. Sometimes you just have to get off your backside and do something and look at what difference it has made.

AR **For example?**

RR In this folder there is a copy of our newsletter; it was started about eighteen months ago. I did another bit of research for us about six months ago to see where our customers were coming from, and they were coming from repeat business. That's not a surprise, but we weren't doing a good job in keeping in touch with those people.

AR **Isn't it funny how that happens?**

RR So I just need something that I can go and put on the desk to let people know that we're there, what is happening, that we regard them as a friend. So we did it, we sent out four hundred. It was very easy, we put the whole thing together and got a professional company to help us, and the response to it has been tremendous.

AR **Really, is it emailed or hard copy?**

RR Hard copy; we're advocates for electronic delivery, but this was impossible to do that way. I know how I view a lot of emails,

I get loads of e-newsletters, and I know what I do with them. I would pick up others I had received through the mail, and look at them for a couple of minutes, fine.

AR   That's interesting. When you're recruiting people as part of continued expansion of the business, I presume you interview before you employ them?

RR   Yes, sometimes it's just me but often it's our project manager.

AR   What do you look for in a candidate when they come to you?

RR   Our business is a people business, it's all about people, it's all about relationships, it's all about being able to engage in a conversation. I've had people phone me up and say ,'I just want to say, I've just been interviewed by one of your researchers and it was a really enjoyable experience,' and it's because those particular people have a skill. It's not about gift of the gab, it's all about being able to listen, and it's about being able to engage in a conversation, and then it's lots of other things like attention to detail, and actually just wanting to do it.

AR   How would someone prove to you that they've got attention to detail at an interview? How can they prove their listening skills?

RR   I think, like a lot of researchers, it's weighing up a body of things. It starts with the cv; we do use a standard application form when we advertise for posts, but we like to see a cv. We like to see some evidence that they have written it themselves and there is some personality coming through. Then it's down to the meeting. Rather than invite them to interviews, we invite them to come in for a chat.

AR   Right, you say that specifically? And what sort of questions do you ask?

RR   We don't tend to go through the cv. I suppose what I'm talking about is researchers and their skills are a bit different to somebody who wants to go out on the street.

AR   There's a lot of those out there, a lot of the readers might do that as their first job.

RR   I speak to loads of people, as you do when networking.

AR **So you think they should listen and obviously have empathy?**

RR Yes. We had a client come down the other day and he said, 'Do you know, it's quite nice to see your research team is not what I was expecting.' I said, 'What do you mean?' and he said, 'Well they're a bit more senior than I would have expected.' We don't tend to recruit loads of students – we do have students if they're the right people, but not if they're phoning us up when they get home saying they can't come in. We need reliability, it speaks volumes.

AR **Good. How do recruits come into your company? Do you advertise?**

RR We have used recruitment agencies for temps, but we tend not to use them now because the commitment isn't there. A lot of our researchers tend to be temporary contracts. We recently advertised for the first time in about ten years. We placed an advert in a local weekly paper and got 130 responses to it!

AR **And you've got to deal with each and every one?**

RR Yes, and we did. We sorted through them and went through a process of elimination. We interviewed 30 and recruited some great people. We set it out as no guaranteed hours. We also recruit through word of mouth; people introduce their relations to us. That proves very successful because somebody's reputation is at stake; you're not going to recommend your sister if you're not confident it's going to work out, so that works well. We have whole families in!

AR **I bet that's very interesting. When it's their first job as a researcher, will they be in the office?**

RR Yes, a lot of it's on the telephone, completing questionnaires. There are all sorts of skills involved in what we do: data collection, telephone quantities research, in-depth interviews, and they all require slightly different skills. In fact somebody who's good at one isn't necessarily good at another. Often our quantities researchers don't make good depth researchers.

AR **And focus groups?**

RR Yes, we do focus groups. We recently did a quantities evaluation on an Objective One Partnership programme, using about eighteen groups across a couple of months. That was working in partnership with another consultancy.

AR **So what else would a recruit expect as their first job in market research, not just with yourself but with other companies? Would research in the city be pretty much the same?**

RR I think if you were in the city you could probably find research work in the evenings. Most of our employees work regular hours and some people come to work for us having done that.

AR **What companies? Does anyone spring to mind for doing that sort of research?**

RR All the big consumer goods companies: telecom companies, mobile phone companies; they are always doing that sort of work.

AR **We haven't yet spoken about graduates. If I was a young graduate looking to go into marketing, particularly market research, what advice would you give me?**

RR Go in at the bottom. Going out on the street with a clip board or sitting on the phone making 150 calls a day doesn't sound like fun, but you've got to go in and learn the trade, so I would start there and get involved. Do as much as you can and really understand it. If you're not already, become a 'people person', that's the best thing you can do. I don't think I could put together research propositions, analyse, or deliver what it means, if I hadn't done my apprenticeship.

AR **The apprenticeship is starting at the bottom?**

RR Yes, I think so, it's the best advice. I suppose there are a lot of marketing graduates out there. I can't advise on the other options available to them, I've not really got involved in our industry as a whole. Being in Cornwall we see ourselves as being of assistance to other companies that use research methodology. There's no point in me going to other research companies, I need to go to other marketing companies and see what problems and challenges they face. I suspect that's a more interesting route into it.

Contact details

Robert Rush
Managing Director, PFA Research Ltd
eCommerce House
7 Lower Bore Street
Bodmin
Cornwall PL31 2JR
Tel: 01208 262000
www.pfa-research.com

Gary Leih, Chairman and Chief Executive, Ogilvy Group UK

Company profile

The Ogilvy Group brings together specialist companies across virtually every communications discipline, including advertising, direct marketing/CRM, PR, sales promotion, design, interactive, media investment, business-to-business, internal communications, healthcare, plus associated studio and creative services operations. With over 474 offices in 120 countries, the Ogilvy Group employs 11,000 people working in 70 languages. The Group's companies work independently as specialists in their own disciplines or in any combination necessary, to integrate campaigns for their clients.

David Ogilvy founded the agency that would later become Ogilvy & Mather, in New York in 1948 and built the company into one of the most prominent and successful advertising networks in the world.

Ogilvy is now owned by WPP, one of the world's largest and most prominent advertising and marketing groups.

Career profile

Leih began his career at Ogilvy, Cape Town in 1980 and progressed through the ranks there and later at Ogilvy, Johannesburg (then South Africa's largest agency), rising to Group Account Director.

In 1989 he co-founded The White House which grew from nothing to become one of the country's hottest agencies, winning Agency of the Year in South Africa in 1991, 1992 and 1993.

In 1994, Leih relocated to Australia where he worked at The Campaign Place and Batey before setting up his own brand consultancy, Public Image, in 1999. Public Image was acquired by TBWA and Leih was Managing Director of TBWA Sydney for two years before returning to Ogilvy Africa in 2001 as Group Managing Director in overall charge of the agency's 1,300 employees.

In May 2005, Gary moved to London to take up the role of Chairman and Chief Executive of the Ogilvy Group UK.

AR   How did you get into marketing and what attracted you to it?

GL   Candidly, I was interested in doing something creative; I did badly in maths in my final year at school and I was keen to become an architect, so the university I applied to said, 'You're going to have to do a year of architectural drafting before we will accept you.'

So I went to study architectural drafting and I did that for a year and decided that I couldn't face drawing cross sections of public works or the whole idea of seven years of study! I dropped out much to my father's disgust and went to sell space on the sides of buses. So I became a commission only employee of a company. I used to call on private businesses and ad agencies try to sell the space

AR   How old were you?

GL   I had just come out of the army – after you have finished school you do a couple of years in the South African army, so I would have been very young. My father told me if I dropped out he wouldn't support me financially so I had to earn money in order to survive.

AR   Were you good at it?

GL   Well I had to be to survive! As I say, I used to call on ad agencies and try and convince them why they should put the products and brands they had in their portfolios on buses, why advertising on buses was fabulous.

At one of the agencies I called upon the media director, who was typically the person I went to see to pitch, said to me 'Why don't you think about joining the "Triple A" advertising course (a postgraduate course), I am sure we can help you to get on to it', which they did. We do a similar thing here at Ogilvy now, but it was a programme which was a year long and they took you through the various aspects of advertising and marketing. You were placed with companies and you had to study at night. It was a great programme with a diploma at the end of it. One of the ad agencies I was placed with offered me a job, and that agency eventually became Ogilvy, although it was an independent agency in those days.

AR   **Did you feel, while doing that first job, that 'this is for me'?**

GL   Absolutely – it was marvellous! Instant! I walked into the agency on the first day and thought 'this is where I want to be'.

AR   **Why? What was the appeal?**

GL   The people, the sense of excitement, the creativity, energy, the youth ... it was enormously appealing.

So I got this position as a trainee account executive and I was put with an ad agency on the VW (Volkswagen) account, and it really was starting at the absolute bottom. You thought that you had become incredibly important being employed, but if someone tells you to go and pick up ten bales of hay for a shoot ... you do it! But it was really good.

I still can't believe we get paid for what we do, honestly! I still feel that way about the business.

AR   **So there were promotions ...?**

GL   Yes, I worked up from an account executive to an account manager and eventually I got to head the VW account for the agency; then they sent me to Johannesburg, which was a much bigger office, and I ended up running about a third of it.

Then the creative director of the agency called me up one day and said 'I am going to start my own agency. Do you want to be a partner?' I was really lucky. He was a bit older, in his mid thirties at that stage, I was 29. So we started an ad agency! We had no clients, no money but we acquired a house which was in quite a strategic position in Cape Town, half way between the edge of town and the 12 Apostle Mountains, 'The White House' (marked on nautical maps as the White House). We bought this old derelict place and made it our company headquarters. We still didn't have a client!

AR   **Was it 'positive youth'?**

GL   Yes, yes – you just wouldn't do that now, too risky. My partners at the time put the money in and bought the house. I had nothing to put in. I had a house and a mortgage against it and two young children ... so you are kind of at the point where you really shouldn't be doing this kind of thing. But I believed implicitly in Mel Miller, the creative partner – a very talented guy, and the other partner, Gerrie Heyneke, was a good sound, financial guy. They had actually got together before me, then I came in as the third partner. So between us it was the right core group to start it: we had someone looking after the money, someone going out looking for the business (me) and someone actually producing the work.

We were very naive and very lucky. We picked up really good business quite quickly, which is the only way to do it; if you don't start with accounts you need to very quickly pick up business, otherwise your cash flow is just not going to allow you to survive.

We were very lucky; we picked up the equivalent of Marks & Spencer, we picked up General Motors, we picked up Bristol Myers. We had to bash the doors down! We created a whole load of collateral materials – brochures and films and stuff – which again we couldn't afford. For General Motors we waited in a hotel where we knew that the CEO was going to be talking. We waited at the lift and jumped in the lift with him, shoved this credentials document in front of him and said: 'we're the guys who have been working for the last seven years on Volkswagen and we are sure you like the Volkswagen advertising better than you like the General Motors advertising – we would love to talk to you...etc etc.' About a week later he phoned us!

AR   **Did he like your presumption?**

GL   I think he did; we got it. So then we opened up a Johannesburg office as we had lots of clients in Jo'Burg, and we did that for about seven or eight years in total.

For three years of those we were Agency of the Year, as judged by the marketing periodicals, for different categories: the Emerging Agency, then the Small Agency, then the Medium Agency. This obviously helped us a lot to get more new business. That was a wonderful, wonderful time.

AR   **From there you went to Australia?**

GL   Yes. There were two issues: one was that we left two years or
      so before the non racial elections and the country was in a hell
      of a mess. We had white extremists saying 'we will stay until the
      last man...', and then there was indiscriminate firing on innocent
      train commuters and bombs at airports.

      The weekend that Chris Hani was assassinated, we were away
      down the coast. Sharon and I went for a walk on the beach on
      the Sunday – these events were all over TV and newspapers
      ... and the girls were very small, so we said, 'We can't take this
      chance – we don't know how it is going to go.' I had also been
      approached by Ogilvy to take up a position in Australia; I kind of
      had this in the back of my mind anyway, so we decided to go.
      So I sold my one-third share of The White House, South Africa.

AR   **Can I bring you back to something you said earlier when
      you said that when you buttonholed the CEO of General
      Motors, he respected your courage in the way you did
      that; would you respect it if someone did that to you?**

GL   I think it is always interesting how people market themselves.
      Some of it comes off and some of it doesn't. But when it does,
      someone does something that is particularly interesting and
      novel, something really catches your eye ... but there must be
      quality there – there is no point in having courage and stunting
      something if there if nothing of quality beneath, because all you
      are going to do is get their attention for a second.

AR   **So people reading this book may be wondering if they
      have what it takes to follow in your footsteps. What
      qualities do you think successful marketers need?**

GL   I think you have got to absolutely love the business and
      believe that advertising can make a difference. You have to
      fundamentally believe in what you are doing. I think there is
      an enormous amount that advertising can do, and does do, to
      aid consumption, economies, growth etc, etc and there is a
      high reward of purpose for advertising.

AR   **Example...?**

GL   One of our clients is Unilever and we do the Dove campaign
      that we originated here in London. I can't claim any credit for it
      because it was done before I arrived, but there is a higher order

role for that Dove campaign – basically, research has shown that 98% of women felt worse about themselves after they read a woman's magazine than they did before they read it, yet they buy them every month! So the stereotypical view that the beauty industry portrays actually undermines people's confidence in themselves.

We thought that we could reverse this and if we had really good, simple products and we talked about the benefits of these products in a very honest and open way. This was a sensation, an absolute sensation! More than 70% of Dove's exposure at that time was absolutely free – it is just PR. Oprah Winfrey devoted an entire show to the Dove campaign! Money just can't buy that.

AR   **Not to do with the product so much as how the customer felt ...**

GL   Yes we tried to show people feeling really comfortable about themselves. How you didn't have to be, or aspire to be, an emaciated catwalk model, in order to feel good about yourself.

So that's what I am talking about and I think even brands like Coca-Cola can make people feel better sometimes. When it does great advertising I think people feel better, they see the world a bit more positively, there is a bit of a lift ...

AR   **So cynical persons shouldn't be marketers?**

GL   Probably not, I think you have to be a pragmatic optimist! You have to love this business. It is about people – we have nothing else. We have a few crayons, but really it is nothing else, just us and our people and their talent.

AR   **So what sort of qualities do you look for in recruits?**

GL   I will explain how it actually happens. We run a three year graduate training programme. It is very intense.

Our grad trainees get the opportunity to work in at least three of 11 companies specialising in different things, PR, design, sales promotion, advertising, CRM, e-CRM and so on. The students of the year before prepare the recruitment data for the next year's students, so it is member get member really. The internet has helped enormously; people are on line, blogging, talking about it ...

We do have people from our human resources department doing presentations at universities and art colleges and that sort of thing. We outreach and for the last year and take on ten people. We had 1,600 qualified applicants – qualified, as in they had some form of tertiary and postgraduate qualification. Its tough.

We also try and look for the odd maverick that hasn't come up that way. I believe there is a lot of talent out there that isn't streamed through the conventional routes. But, to be honest, that is the exception rather than the rule now.

These kids are bright! A lot of them have read English, history, political science and may have done a postgraduate in journalism, law or marketing.

The graduates go through a rigorous programme. They write essays, some fun some serious, from 'the role of advertising in a free enterprise economy' to 'if you were brand Madonna, what would you do now to reinvent yourself?' We test their logic and their 'magic'. We sift, sift, during around 200–300 face to face interviews. It is intensive. Each person is interviewed twice by two different people, and they are all scored. The last 50 do a two-day workshop where they work with our people and we get a sense of chemistry and a measure of them.

AR   **Do you get involved in this?**

GL   I present to all the shortlist and talk face-to-face to the last 50, get a sense of who they are and then we will choose our annual intake of ten. We have thirty graduates in the building at different stages of their development – some of them in their first year, some second year, some third year. They are terrific people. They bind together very well. We make them do a lot of basic stuff. For instance on the inter-agency rugby day they set up the tents, they have to muck in which is great.

It is not easy now. For me it feels, frankly, more competitive, harder than it has ever been to get into our business.

AR   **Do other advertising agencies run programmes?**

GL   Yes. Our parent company WPP runs one as well. I think BBH (Bartle Bogle Hegarty), I think AMV (Abbot Mead Vickers) and others do.

AR   **And are there other routes into the industry ...?**

GL   It is extremely difficult to get in any other way if you have come straight out of university. But with some experience in a related field you may be able to get in, but its tough. Recently we took on someone who had been in book publishing and was a very good copywriter; these are rare, once they have made a name for themselves, they earn very good money. I'd rather grow our own copywriters than steal other peoples'.

AR   **Is there a self employed route?**

GL   Yes, with experience its possible – there is no reason why not.

AR   **Does it still happen?**

GL   Yes – we would love to see it happen more, frankly. New start-up agencies keep you on your toes! As you mature as an agency, you take on more and more blue chip type business with big and mature brands: the IBMs, American Expresses and Barclays of this world ... The small agencies can also develop talent which can migrate.

AR   **Can you think of a small agency campaign which we would know?**

GL   Have you come across a brand call Innocent Smoothies? That is done by a small agency. A lovely campaign.

AR   **What would you say to someone who wants to be in advertising?**

GL   Never give up. Just that – tenacity is everything! It is, honestly, 99% perspiration, getting into this business ... you are going to have to cope with rejection, really cope, keep knocking and keep pushing at the door if you want to get anywhere in this business.

AR   **Do agencies with blue chip clients loose the edge?**

GL   I think there are definitely life cycles but the best agencies keep sharp. You have to.

    Clients want magic. They don't need us for anything other than to come up with a really compelling idea that can help drive their brand forward. We know how to support and encourage creative people – we have learnt how to create a special environment for them. We need sharp young minds in order to stay sharp as a business. In fact that is our business.

AR　**Do you do your own research?**

GL　We do some ourselves but mostly our clients want independent research to validate the point of view that we proffer.

AR　**So are you interested in research?**

GL　Yes, but we do a lot of consumer research around attitudes, trends ... we try and do a lot of future casting so we have a big planning department. I think we have about 60 planners who try to map out a way forward for client brands to follow. We have a whole bunch of people dealing with many outside institutions – like the London School of Economics – so we can advise, and explain what we actually think is going to happen in the marketplace. They (clients) can go outside to other specialised consultancies for this type of thing, but we try to give some kind of sense of future too.

AR　**Are there other departments that take on marketers?**

GL　Yes – within the ad agency you have Client Services itself, which is the background I grew up in, so basically running the account, interfacing with the client; Planning, which as I was explaining is strategic communications planning; then you have Creative, which is normally broken up into Art Direction and Writing. We have Television Production, we have Print Production and every type of media production in this agency.

AR　**So each of the 11 Ogilvy parts does its own thing; with different recruitment procedures?**

GL　Yes, each of our companies has an HR function, manager and department. In addition, at a group level we conduct the Graduate Trainee Programme with an overall head of recruitment.

AR　**Last question! You have had a great career – what has been the worst bit and the best bit?**

GL　Worst bit would probably be giving up my own agency – that was the most difficult thing I have ever done in my life – period – not just career. To actually walk away from something you have created from scratch after seven or eight years and to get on a plane to another country. Very difficult!

The best part was getting my first job in advertising. When I got a phone call to say 'we would like to offer you a job as an account executive' was the best day of my advertising career – if not one of the best days of my life (so far).

Contact details

Ogilvy Group
10 Cobalt Square
Canary Wharf
London
E14 4QB
Tel: 020 7345 3000
www.ogilvy.com

....

Juliet Kosta, Events Organiser

Personal profile

Juliet is a very meticulous marketing professional. She most recently worked in Bristol and now works for a luxury hotel in the West Country as an events organiser.

AR **We are interested in marketing people; could you give us a 'job description'?**

JK   I have been an events organiser for three different companies. The first thing you have to do is to assess the existing marketing approach. I have always had to first update images, brochure packs, materials, that kind of thing.

Then when a client rings you must give them a personal immediate response. That is key – they don't want an email, or something in the post ... you should listen very carefully to what someone is telling you and then give, if possible, exactly what they want!

It's a good idea to keep records, enquiry source, social info demographics, how they found you for example. Things like contact details, postcode, how they got our number – internet or have been recommended to you. You keep and use this information all the time.

You then always follow up your first response. If they don't want to use your services, try to find out why – but there are only so many times you can call someone, if you have left four messages they are just not interested!

You then have an onsite meeting to find out what people want to spend on hotel functions, and no deposits are taken until a project outline is agreed. Everyone signs a contract, so there are no surprises: you don't want to know the day before the wedding that the budget is £30,000, you need to know the year before.

Then you produce a very detailed brief with contact names, times and so on. It needs to be really, really precise: if they have a wedding cake and they want the second half of the second tier saved and posted to grandma in Australia, you have to make sure that is written down.

When you are an events organiser you have to print every single email received and sent because if, six months down the line they say 'no, no, no, you said £17.99', you need to prove that you wrote and said it was £X.

You have to liaise with lots of different parties. You have to be very organised and must be good at multi-tasking. A good memory helps – people phone you up and say 'Hi, it's Julie!' and you have to know exactly which one out of a possible twenty Julies, is calling you.

On the day itself you have to have a real presence and appear to be very calm, that nothing is too much trouble even if behind the scenes you want to scream!

AR **So what attracted you to marketing in the first place?**

JK When I first thought of event management I didn't consider it to be a marketing role, but I know now that it very much is. We sell a service and I love this job. It comes naturally to me and I found that I was good at it and enjoyed it – very much the job that I was aiming for at the start of my career.

AR **Can you describe your previous jobs?**

JK I worked for one company who had two very different venues: one was a 1920s glass restaurant boat permanently moored in

Bristol, and one was a huge converted, cavernous night club/ restaurant with a Moroccan décor, very different.

I loved that job! My office was on the boat, city centre, quite glamorous, lots of BBC events, it paid me a lot of money and I worked hard.

In my current role I work in a small luxury hotel group – the highest revenue is the wedding business – very country house, very English high quality service.

AR   So how did you get your first job?

JK   I was head-hunted, they interviewed me and ten minutes later said, 'We are going to go a bit 'off-piste' here, can you come and do this?'... they had seen me in action when I was running a restaurant.

AR   What is the best bit of your current role?

JK   Managing my own diary. You don't clock in or clock out and I do enjoy that and have to be organised – its not a 9 to 5 job so I've become a big list maker, quite methodical. You have to be quite industrious. You have to get your head down and get on with it. But then, when you are done, you leave!

AR   What is the worst bit?

JK   Working every Saturday and Sunday in the season.

AR   What do you look forward to when you get up in the morning?

JK   On the marketing side of it, it is ticking boxes, getting the bookings in, hitting the projected sales targets and contributing significantly to the company's profit margin. That sort of thing. I love doing a good job and getting thank you cards, mainly from the weddings: 'Oh, we couldn't have done it without you, it has been amazing, we will remember the day forever' ... that's great!

AR   What sort of personal qualities does someone reading this book need to have to make a success in marketing?

JK   Common sense. You need to instantly be able to adapt your persona to fit the bill. For example, if you have a customer who wants to celebrate a wedding anniversary but wants things kept simple – just do that. If they don't want champagne and canapés don't offer them.

AR **So it helps if you can understand what people want quickly?**

JK Yes, you need to alter your pitch and your personality to suit the customer. In marketing it helps if you can be a social chameleon and you have to be able to think on your feet, make clients feel comfortable, at ease.

You must also know your product inside and out. For example, today I have a meeting with someone from the NHS who has taken out a day to visit a number of venues, so if she says 'Could you get 40 people in this room with a projector with a U-shaped table and so on..' you have to know straight away. If you can't offer them what they want it's OK to say so. Never be afraid of saying 'no' because you are the one there promising things, and if on the day it doesn't get delivered you are in trouble.

AR **When you recruit people for marketing what sort of impression do they need to make?**

JK Be punctual – without fail! If you walk into the room your audience must sit up, and take notice when you announce who you are. You must shake hands warmly, try to answer questions clearly and be precise, that sort of thing.

AR **Anything else?**

JK They would need to look the part – if it was a guy coming to my hotel, for example, he would not need to be in a black suit, but perhaps in casual but smart with a tie – that sort of thing. You must dress to suit the environment you are going to work in, you have to look good! Instant first impressions do count. Everybody does it – you judge a book by its cover.

AR **So during the interview how would someone impress you?**

JK Someone who is not too cocky; doesn't glorify themselves; knows their stuff; asks and answers questions and is someone who I feel I could get on with; someone who I would buy something from.

AR **Confident?**

JK Yes, but not start every conversation with 'I'!

AR **... if they want to know something they need to feel able to ask more?**

JK   Yes, absolutely. And if they don't understand something to ask 'can you just tell me what you mean by that' rather than just nodding at everything and then being caught out later.

Contact details

Write to Juliet c/o andi@startupbiz.org

Conclusion

My father ran a garage and thought I should learn the ropes. As a result the garage foreman was given the job teaching me the rudiments of mechanical engineering every Saturday morning. I think at best I could have been described as a reluctant car mechanic.

I remember lying on my back in the dirt underneath a car and for some obscure reason suddenly getting covered in oil. Not fresh oil you understand, but the sort of oil that has been doing whatever job it is that oil does for several years, so that it carried with it the weight, smell and grime of time. I remember Adrian, my Dad's right-hand man, barely concealing laughter as a peculiar, overall-clad black-and-white minstrel emerged blinking from under the car.

'You're just not enjoying this are you Andi?' he said, choking on his mirth 'Shall I tell your Dad or will you?'

It was with an air of resignation rather than disappointment that my father received the news of my mechanical ineptitude, and my desire to go to London to look for what he referred to as 'non-existent paving stones of gold'.

My father was right; there were no golden paving stones. However, I did find a way of making a living that did not involve getting covered in oil.

One Autumn day I strolled into a busy office. It was clean and full of life and exciting, it was 1981. My first colleagues, an ex-major of the Guards regiment, an ex-milkman from South London, the ex-Mayor of Greenwich and a charming blue blooded socialite called Bevan, and the whole place was run effortlessly by a charming lady called Sue, the manager's PA. I knew straight away that although I had a great deal to learn, I had found my niche.

I'd gone to London for the weekend and stayed there for ten years. One day my father noticed I'd not been around much and called me. 'How's things going up there in London?' he asked. 'OK, Phil and I have bought a house!' I said, to a choking sound on other end of the phone. I was 22. It was 1982 and I was having the time of my life.

Now it's 2009 and I'm writing this epilogue and you are reading it. It feels odd coming to the end of the book. I have found myself remembering all sorts of things as I look back over a 30 year career in sales and marketing.

Marketing is a great place to be if you like people and enjoy a creative challenge in a commercial environment. I am reminded once again of the jaundiced view of marketing that my mum had at first. She soon changed her mind about marketing when she realised how much fun I was having making a good living. 'No froth, no fizz!' she would say, smiling after the incident I described at the beginning of this book.

I do hope that this book answers a few questions and helps you make the right decision for you. It's been fun writing it.

So there it is. If you're reading this you are contemplating a career in marketing. If you become a marketer you're going to encounter your share of highs and lows, but the bottom line is you are never going to be lonely, you are never going to be bored and, most importantly, there's always going to be a new challenge around the corner. If you like the sound of that you're going to love marketing.

Resources

PROFESSIONAL ORGANISATIONS

American Marketing Association for Information and resources: www. marketingpower.com

British Market Research Association: www.bmra.org.uk

British Market Research Bureau: www.bmrb.co.uk, Tel: 020 8433 4000

Chartered Institute of Marketing: www.cim.co.uk, Tel: 01628 427120/427130

resources: http://livebeta.cim.co.uk/resources/home.aspx

training and qualifications: http://livebeta.cim.co.uk/tandq/home.aspx

Communications Advertising and Marketing Education Foundation: www. camfoundation.com

Direct Marketing Association (UK) Ltd: www.dma.org.uk, Tel: 020 7291 3300

Direct Selling Association (DSA): www.dsa.org.uk

Institute of Direct Marketing: www.theidm.com

Institute of Sales and Marketing Management: www.ismm.co.uk

Institute of Sales Promotion: www.isp.org.uk

Internet Advertising Bureau (UK): www.iabuk.net

Market Research Society: www.mrs.org.uk, Tel: 020 7490 4911

Marketing and Sales Standards Setting Body: www.msssb.org

Marketing Science Institute: www.msi.org

Marketing Society: www.marketing-society.org.uk

Office of National Statistics: www.ons.gov.uk

ONLINE RESOURCES

For practical know-how and case studies: www.marketingsherpa.com

For the latest proven tips and tricks, success stories, latest news and commentary: http://marketing.briefme.com

Brand Republic: www.brandrepublic.com. This site is the starting
point for links to lots of information, online forums and e-versions of
Haymarket's titles.

Graduate Recruitment Bureau: www.grb.uk.com

www.mad.co.uk: delivers business insight to professionals in marketing,
media, new media, advertising and design.

Marketing: marketingmagazine.co.uk; marketing industry, including
media, retail and direct marketing. Online, you can find marketing's top
100 agencies and companies.

www.marketingchannel.co.uk: this site is home to a series of publications
and events for the marketing industry, which are designed to show the
cost-effective use of measurable marketing channels to best effect.

Marketing Direct: www.marketingdirectmag.co.uk; direct marketing. The
website has blogs from a range of leading industry commentators.

Promotions & Incentives: www.promotionsandincentives.co.uk;
promotional marketing sector.

Revolution: www.revolutionmagazine.com; digital marketing in the UK.
Digital news can be found on its website, as well as a blog.

MAGAZINES

Campaign (weekly) www.campaignlive.co.uk
Marketing Magazine (weekly) www.marketingmagazine.co.uk
Marketing Today: www.marketingtoday.com
Marketing Week (weekly) www.marketingweek.co.uk
Media Week (weekly) www.mediaweek.co.uk
The Marketer (CIM) www.themarketer.co.uk
Find others at: www.world-newspapers.com/marketing-magazines.html

QUALIFICATIONS AND TRAINING

http://careersadvice.direct.gov.uk
CIM qualifications advice: www.cim.co.uk/tandq/home.aspx
Connexions Direct: www.connexions-direct.com
Department of Employment and Learning Northern Ireland: www.delni.
gov.uk
Highlands and Islands Enterprise: www.hie.co.uk

Learn Direct: www.learndirect.co.uk, helpline 0800 101 901
Learning Aims Database: http://providers.lsc.gov.uk/lad/default.asp
Learning and Skills Council: www.lsc.gov.uk
Llywodraeth Cynulliad Cymru, Welsh Assembly Government: http://new.
    wales.gov.uk/?lang=en
Marketing and Sales Standard Setting Body: www.msssb.org
QCA (national database of accredited qualifications): www.
    accreditedqualifications.org.uk
Scottish Enterprise: www.scottish-enterprise.com
SQA - Scottish Qualification Authority: www.sqa.org.uk/sqa
www.thegraduate.co.uk
Train 2 Gain: www.traintogain.gov.uk
UCAS: www.ucas.com

WORK EXPERIENCE

www.myinternship.co.uk
www.nus.org.uk/en/student-life/Careers-Advice/How-to-get-
    experience-in/
www.work-experience.org
www.work-placement.co.uk

SUGGESTED INTRODUCTORY BOOKS

D. Adcock, A. Halborg & C. Ross, *Marketing: Principles and Practice*,
    Prentice Hall, 2001
Gary Armstrong, Philip Kotler, *Marketing an Introduction* (5th edn), US:
    Prentice Hall, 2000
Michael J Baker (for CIM), *Marketing Manual*, UK: Butterworth
    Heinemann, 1998
Michael J Baker, *Marketing: An Introductory Text* (7th edn), Helensburgh:
    2006
Jim Blythe, *Principles and Practice of Marketing*, London: Thompson
    Learning, 2006
Jim Blythe, *Essentials of Marketing* (4th edn), Harlow: Financial Times/
    Prentice Hall, 2008
Frances Brassington, Stephen Pettitt, *Essentials of Marketing* (2nd edn),
    Harlow: Financial Times/Prentice Hall, 2007

Elizabeth Hill, Terry O'Sullivan, *Foundation Marketing* (3rd edn), Harlow: Financial Times/Prentice Hall, 2004

Elizabeth Hill, Terry O'Sullivan, *Introductory Certificate in Marketing: CIM Companion*, Cookham: CIM Publishing, 2004

Philip Kotler, *Marketing Management: Analysis, Planning, Implementation and Control*. (6th edn) Upper Saddle River: Prentice Hall, 1988

Philip Kotler, *Marketing Insights from A to Z: 80 Concepts Every Manager Needs to Know*, Hoboken: Wiley, 2003

Geoffrey Lancaster, Paul Reynolds, *Introduction to Marketing: A Step by Step Guide to All the Tools of Marketing*, London: Kogan Page, 1999

Geoffrey Lancaster, Paul Reynolds, *Marketing Made Simple*, Oxford: Made Simple, 2002

David Ogilvy, *An Autobiography*, London: Hamish Hamilton, 1978

David Ogilvy, *Confessions of an Advertising Man*, London: Scribner Book Company, 1980

William Perreault, E J McCarthy, *Basic Marketing: A Global Managerial Approach* (14th international edn), Burr Ridge, Ilinois, US: McGraw-Hill, 2002

Harshani Samarajeewa, *Marketing Made Easy,* Sri Lanka: Swisscontact, 1999